VISIBLE
LEARNING
FOR LITERACY
GRADES K–12

VISIBLE LEARNING FOR LITERACY

Implementing the
Practices That Work
Best to Accelerate
Student Learning

GRADES K–12

DOUGLAS FISHER · NANCY FREY · JOHN HATTIE

FOR INFORMATION:

Corwin

A SAGE Company

2455 Teller Road

Thousand Oaks, California 91320

(800) 233-9936

www.corwin.com

SAGE Publications Ltd.

1 Oliver's Yard

55 City Road

London EC1Y 1SP

United Kingdom

SAGE Publications India Pvt. Ltd.

B 1/I 1 Mohan Cooperative Industrial Area

Mathura Road, New Delhi 110 044

India

SAGE Publications Asia-Pacific Pte. Ltd.

3 Church Street

#10-04 Samsung Hub

Singapore 049483

Publisher: Lisa Luedeke

Editorial Development Manager: Julie Nemer

Editorial Assistant: Nicole Shade

Production Editor: Melanie Birdsall

Copy Editor: Melinda Masson

Typesetter: C&M Digitals (P) Ltd.

Proofreader: Alison Syring

Indexer: Sheila Bodell

Cover Designer: Rose Storey

Marketing Manager: Rebecca Eaton

Printed in the United States of America

Library of Congress Cataloging-in-Publication Data

Names: Fisher, Douglas, author. | Frey, Nancy, author. | Hattie, John, author.

Title: Visible learning for literacy, grades K–12 : implementing the practices that work best to accelerate student learning / Douglas Fisher, Nancy Frey, John Hattie.

Description: Thousand Oaks, California : Corwin/A SAGE Company, 2016. | Includes bibliographical references and index.

Identifiers: LCCN 2015048505 | ISBN 9781506332352 (pbk. : alk. paper)

Subjects: LCSH: Language arts (Elementary) | Language arts (Secondary) | Literacy—Study and teaching (Elementary) | Literacy—Study and teaching (Secondary) | Visual learning.

Classification: LCC LB1576 .F338 2016 | DDC 372.6—dc23 LC record available at http://lccn.loc.gov/2015048505

This book is printed on acid-free paper.

Certified Chain of Custody
Promoting Sustainable Forestry
www.sfiprogram.org
SFI-01268

SFI label applies to text stock

16 17 18 19 20 10 9 8 7 6 5 4

Contents

Visit the companion website at
http://resources.corwin.com/VL-Literacy
to access videos and downloadable versions
of all reproducibles.

List of Videos

Note From the Publisher: The authors have provided video and web content throughout the book that is available to you through QR (quick response) codes. To read a QR code, you must have a smartphone or tablet with a camera. We recommend that you download a QR code reader app that is made specifically for your phone or tablet brand.

Videos may also be accessed at
http://resources.corwin.com/VL-Literacy.

(Continued)

Preface

Literacy educators have been in search of "what works" for decades. As a group, we've dedicated ourselves to students' reading and writing (and speaking, listening, and viewing) development because we know that literacy can change lives. Our collective search for better ways to reach students and ensure that they develop literacy knowledge and skills has resulted in thousands and thousands of books, hundreds of thousands of research articles, and countless websites. So why another one?

For us, the answer is simple. Nearly all the things teachers do work when we ask what improves student achievement. But only a few things work at ensuring that students gain a full year's worth of growth for a year of enrollment in school, and we think it's time we focused on what works, what doesn't work, and what can't hurt. And we've turned to *Visible Learning* (Hattie, 2009) for help.

In part, this has been a personal journey. We (Nancy and Doug) engaged in literacy instruction in a wide range of settings, including preschools, elementary schools, middle schools, and high schools, for many years before we read *Visible Learning*. We have taught students who live in poverty, a wide range of English learners, students who are highly engaged in their own learning, students who are homeless, students with disabilities, students who grasp concepts almost instantly, and students who are not so motivated to be in school. Over the years, our classrooms have been wonderfully diverse and complex places for learning to occur. And we did a reasonably good job with developing students' literacy.

Of course, we made mistakes as well, but all teachers do. Doug wishes he could find Anthony, a ninth grader from 2009, who just never got good enough writing instruction to pass his classes. Today, Doug would do a better job. Nancy remembers a particular first grader who would only work on his onset and rime cards if Nancy played background music. Whatever it takes—that's the job of the teacher. We tried just about any instructional strategy that we could find to engage students in learning.

But then, along came *Visible Learning*. We've read the research, and we knew, for example, that vocabulary instruction works to improve student learning. We read the book and were pleased to see that many of the literacy approaches we recommended were included in this list of "what works best." We congratulated ourselves on knowing the research literature and trying to translate that into classroom practice. The list of effect sizes was useful in making the case that literacy educators can have a powerful impact on students' learning when they engage in specific actions. And it was useful to know that a great deal of students' learning was under the control of the teacher (so that we could help teachers take responsibility and reduce finger-pointing).

We started focusing on influences on student learning that had a reasonable impact. But we didn't have them organized in any particular way. As a result, we noticed that not all of these approaches worked equally well. We thought it had to be us because the research was there to support each of the routines we used. We weren't sure what to do, so we kept at it, engaging students in the best learning opportunities we could. We shared responsibility with them and guided their learning, such that more and more of our students became their own teachers, which is one of the major lessons learned from *Visible Learning*.

A chance encounter with John Hattie took us to the next level. John talked about the value of matching specific instructional routines, procedures, or strategies with the appropriate phase of students' learning. Of course, we knew about Bloom's taxonomy and Webb's depth of knowledge. But this was a bit different. John said that students have to develop surface-level learning if they are ever going to go deep. And we know that deep learning can facilitate transfer, which has been our goal all along.

So we updated our lessons and started thinking about which instructional routines worked at the surface level. With our colleagues, we focused on some specific instructional approaches early in units of study, when students needed to expand their surface-level skills. And then, importantly, we stopped using these procedures when students moved into deeper learning. And it worked. We all had more students, more often, engaged in deeper learning. And students were transferring their learning from class to class, grade to grade, and year to year.

So there we sat, realizing that it was time to write another book. This time, we needed to explore the ways in which the *Visible Learning* influences could be mobilized at three levels—surface, deep, and transfer. And who better to collaborate with than John Hattie himself? Together, we hoped that the literacy world might be open to rethinking strategies and shifting focus to the alignment of these strategies in tune with phases of learning.

The result is this book that you're holding right now. It's our best thinking to date about being an effective literacy educator. Knowing how to match instructional approaches with specific phases of learning, knowing your impact, and taking action when the impact is not sufficient has become our newest and most robust effort to help students inherit the world of literacy.

Acknowledgments

Corwin gratefully acknowledges the contributions of the following reviewers:

Leslie Blauman
Teacher, Consultant,
    and Corwin Author
Cherry Creek School District
Denver, CO

Marisa Burvikovs
Talent Development Teacher
LaGrange District 102
Brookfield, IL

Deb Cale
Curriculum Coordinator
Johnston Schools
Johnston, IA

Amy Korst
Language Arts Teacher
    and Adjunct Faculty
Willamina High School and
    Western Oregon University
Willamina and Monmouth, OR

Michael Rafferty
Director of Teaching
    and Learning
Region 14 School District
Woodbury, CT

Terrell Tracy
Director of EdS in Literacy,
    Assistant Professor
    of Education
Converse College
Spartanburg, SC

Daniel Winters
Principal
Camarena Elementary School
Chula Vista Elementary
    School District
Chula Vista, CA

LAYING THE GROUNDWORK FOR VISIBLE LEARNING FOR LITERACY

1

Every student deserves a great teacher, not by chance, but by design.

Who can disagree with that? Who doesn't believe that every student, in every classroom, deserves to be educated in ways that build his or her confidence and competence? Let's take apart that sentence and explore some of the thinking behind each word or phrase.

- *Every student* (not just some students, such as those whose parents can afford it or those who are lucky enough to live on a street that allows them to attend an amazing school)

- *deserves* (yes, we believe that students have the right to a quality education)

- *a great teacher* (one who develops strong relationships, knows his or her content and how to teach it, and evaluates his or her impact. This is where a lot of debate enters the picture because people differ in their understanding of what great teachers do and how they think)

- *not by chance* (meaning that we have to move beyond the luck of the draw that permeates much of the educational landscape. Children's education should not be left to chance, with one year being amazing and another average or awful. Further, children's education should be left not to whatever sense of challenge or level of expectation a teacher may have, but to an appropriate high level of challenge and expectation)

- *but by design* (yes, there are learning designs that work, when used at the right time. In fact, the literature is awash with evidence of designs that work and those that do not work)

The design we're talking about, the one that has great potential for impacting students' learning and allowing all of us to be great teachers, is John Hattie's *Visible Learning* (2009). So what do we mean by *visible learning*? In part, it's about developing an understanding of the impact that instructional efforts have on students' learning. Notice we didn't limit that to teachers. Students, teachers, parents, administrators—everyone can determine if the learning is visible. To do so, students have to know what they are learning, why they are learning it, what it means to be "good" at this learning, and what it means to have learned. The adults *also* need to know what students are learning, why they are learning it, what it means to be "good" at this learning, and what it means to have learned. Some things are learned at the surface level, others at the deep level, and still other knowledge is available for transfer to new situations. Each of these surface, deep, and transfer levels of learning is important; each of these is the focus, in turn, of one of the following three chapters.

We believed that it was time to apply John's previous work with visible learning to the world of literacy learning. We think that visible learning for *literacy* is important for several reasons:

1. Literacy is among the major antidotes for poverty.

2. Literacy makes your life better.

3. Literate people have more choices in their work and personal lives, leading to greater freedom.

4. Literacy is great at teaching you how to think successively—that is, making meaning one step at a time to then build a story.

5. Literacy soon becomes the currency of other learning.

Visible learning for literacy requires that teachers understand which strategies and instructional routines are useful in which teaching situations. There is no single right way to develop students' literacy prowess. But there *are* wrong ways. In Chapter 5, we will turn our attention to a specific list of practices that do not work in the literacy classroom. For now, we will focus on those that do.

There are certain things that great teachers know:

- Great teachers understand that different approaches work more effectively at different times. For example, a great approach for developing students' surface-level learning is not likely to ensure deep learning, much less transfer. But there are times when their surface-level learning is what students need.

- Great teachers know that different approaches work for some students better than for other students.

- Great teachers know that different approaches work differently depending on where in the learning process a student may be.

- Great teachers intervene in specific, meaningful, and calculated ways to increase students' learning trajectories. This requires that they understand and share challenging, yet specific and appropriate, goals with students; monitor progress toward those goals; provide and receive feedback; alter their actions when learning is not occurring; and share in the joy that comes from working with students to meet the learning goals.

Visible learning asks teachers to go even a step further. It asks us to create the conditions necessary for students to become *their own* teachers. We mean not that classrooms should be surrendered and the students be told to teach themselves, but rather that the expectation of the instruction students receive involves student engagement to the degree that they want to, and do, learn more and better—even beyond the classroom walls. This requires that teachers become learners of their own teaching, which is the major focus of this book.

The Evidence Base

Meta-Analyses

The starting point for our exploration of literacy learning is John Hattie's books, *Visible Learning* (2009) and *Visible Learning for Teachers* (2012). At the time these books were published, his work was based on over 800 meta-analyses conducted by researchers all over the world, which included over 50,000 individual studies that included over 250 million students. It has been claimed to be the most comprehensive review of literature ever conducted. And the thing is, it's still going on. At the time of this writing, the database included 1,200 meta-analyses, with over 70,000 studies and 300 million students. A lot of data, right? But the story underlying the data is the critical matter.

Before we explore the findings and discuss what we don't cover in this book, we should discuss the idea of a meta-analysis because it is the basic building block for the recommendations in this book. At its root, a meta-analysis is a statistical tool for combining findings from different studies with the goal of identifying patterns that can inform practice. It's the old preponderance of evidence that we're looking for, because individual studies have a hard time making a compelling case for change. But a meta-analysis synthesizes what is currently known about a given topic and can result in strong recommendations about the impact or effect of a specific practice. For example, there was competing evidence about periodontitis (inflammation of the tissue around the teeth) and whether or not it is associated with increased risk of coronary heart disease. The published evidence contained some conflicts, and recommendations about treatment were piecemeal. A meta-analysis of 5 prospective studies with 86,092 patients suggested that individuals with periodontitis had a 1.14 times higher risk of developing coronary heart disease than the controls (Bahekar, Singh, Saha, Molnar, & Arora, 2007). The result of the meta-analysis was a set of clear recommendations for treatment of periodontitis, with the potential of significantly reducing the incidence of heart disease. We won't tell you too many other stories about health care or business, but we hope that the value of meta-analyses in changing practice is clear.

The statistical approach for conducting meta-analyses is beyond the scope of this book, but it is important to note that this tool allows researchers to identify trends across many different studies and their participants.

Effect Sizes

In addition to the meta-analyses, the largest summary of educational research ever conducted (*Visible Learning*) contains *effect sizes* for each practice (see Appendix, pages 169–173). An effect size is the magnitude, or size, of a given effect. But defining a phrase by using the same terms isn't that helpful. So we'll try again. You might remember from your statistics class that studies report statistical significance. Researchers make the case that something "worked" when chance is reduced to 5% (as in $p < 0.05$) or 1% (as in $p < 0.01$)—what they really mean is that the effect found in the study was unlikely to be zero: something happened (but there's no hint of the size of the effect, or whether it was worthwhile!).

One way to increase the likelihood that statistical significance is reached is to increase the number of people in the study, also known as sample size. We're not saying that researchers inflate the size of the research group to obtain significant findings. We are saying that simply because something is statistically significant doesn't mean it's worth implementing. For example, say the sample size is 1,000. In this case, a correlation only needs to exceed 0.044 to be "statistically significant"; if 10,000, then 0.014, and if 100,000, then 0.004—yes, you can be confident that these values are greater than zero, but are they of any practical value?

That's where effect size comes in.

Effect size represents the magnitude of the impact that a given approach has.

Say, for example, that this amazing writing program was found to be statistically significant in changing student achievement. Sounds good, you say to yourself, and you consider purchasing or adopting it. But then you learn that it only increased students' writing performance by 0.3 on a 5-point rubric (and the research team had data from 9,000 students). If it were free and easy to implement this change, it might be worth it to have students get a tiny bit better as writers. But if it were time-consuming, difficult, or expensive, you should ask yourself if it's worth it to go to all of this trouble for such a small gain. That's effect size—it represents the magnitude of the impact that a given approach has.

EFFECT SIZE FOR DIRECT INSTRUCTION = 0.59

Visible Learning provides readers with effect sizes for many influences under investigation. As an example, direct instruction has a reasonably strong effect size at 0.59 (we'll talk more about what the effect size number tells us in the next section). The effect sizes can be ranked from those with the highest impact to those with the lowest. But that doesn't mean that teachers should just take the top 10 or 20 and try to implement them immediately. Rather, as we will discuss later in this book, some of the highly useful practices are more effective when focused on surface-level learning while others work better for deep learning and still others work to encourage transfer. Purpose, context, and timing of practices all matter and must be considered. For general discussion of effect sizes, see Figure 1.1.

A PRIMER ON EFFECT SIZES

Let us get a sense of what an effect size means. There are two common ways to calculate an effect size: first, when two groups are compared—such as comparing a class receiving a literacy program with a similar class not receiving this program—and second, over time—such as comparing the performance of a group of students at the outset and again at the end of a series of literacy instruction. In both cases, the effect size represents the magnitude of the difference—and of course the quality of the comparison, the measuring instruments, and the research design to control extraneous factors are critical.

An effect size of $d = 0.0$ indicates no change in achievement related to the intervention. An effect size of $d = 1.0$ indicates an increase of one standard deviation on the outcome (e.g., reading achievement), a $d = 1.0$ increase is typically associated with advancing children's achievement by two to three years, and this would mean that, on average, the achievement of students receiving the treatment would exceed that of 84% of students not receiving the treatment. Cohen (1988) argued that an effect size of d = 1.0 should be regarded as a large, blatantly obvious, and grossly perceptible difference, and as an example, he referred to the difference between the average IQ of PhD graduates and high school students. Another example is the difference between a person at 5'3" (160 cm) and one at 6'0" (183 cm)—which would be a difference visible to the naked eye.

We do need to be careful about ascribing adjectives such as *small, medium,* and *large* to these effect sizes. Cohen (1988), for example, suggested that $d = 0.2$ was small, $d = 0.5$ medium, and $d = 0.8$ large, whereas it is possible to show that when investigating achievement influences in schools, $d = 0.2$ could be considered small, $d = 0.4$ medium, and $d = 0.6$ large (Hattie, 2009). In many cases, this attribution would be reasonable, but there are situations where this would be too simple an interpretation. Consider, for example, the effects of an influence such as behavioral objectives, which has an overall small effect of $d = 0.20$, and reciprocal teaching, which has an overall large effect of $d = 0.74$. It may be that the cost of implementing behavioral objectives is so small that it is worth using them to gain an influence on achievement, albeit small, whereas it might be too expensive to implement reciprocal teaching to gain the larger effect.

The relation between the notions of magnitude and statistical significance is simple: Significance = Effect size × Study size. This should highlight why both aspects are important when making judgments. Effect sizes based on small samples or small numbers of studies may not tell the true story, in the same way that statistical significance based on very large samples may also not tell the true story (for example, a result could be statistically significant but have only a tiny effect size). Similarly, two studies with the same effect sizes can have different implications when their sample sizes vary (we should place more weight on the one based on the larger sample size). The most critical aspect of any study is the convincibility of the story that best explains the data; it is the visible learning story that needs critique or improvement—to what degree is the story in this book convincing to you?

Figure 1.1

The effect size of direct instruction doesn't mean that classrooms should be composed of all direct instruction any more than they should be fully cooperative versus individualistic (which has an effect size of 0.59). Direct instruction likely works better during surface-level literacy learning whereas cooperative learning can deepen students' understanding of content (provided that students have sufficient surface knowledge to then make relations and extend ideas). Both can be effective when used for the right purpose. The effect size list also includes some things that don't work.

> EFFECT SIZE FOR COOPERATIVE VERSUS INDIVIDUALISTIC LEARNING = 0.59

Noticing What Works

If you attend any conference or read just about any professional journal, not to mention subscribe to blogs or visit Pinterest, you'll get the sense that everything works. Yet educators have a lot to learn from practices that do not work. In fact, we would argue that learning from what doesn't work, and not repeating those mistakes, is a valuable use of time. To determine what doesn't work, we turn our attention to effect sizes again. Effect sizes can be negative or positive, and they scale from low to high. Intuitively, an effect size of 0.60 is better than an effect size of 0.20. Intuitively, we should welcome any effect that is greater than zero—as zero means "no growth" and clearly any negative effect size means a negative growth. If only it was this simple.

It turns out that about 95%+ of the influences that we use in schools have a positive effect; that is, the effect size of nearly everything we do is greater than zero. This helps explain why so many people can argue "with evidence" that their pet project works. If you set the bar at showing any growth above zero, it is indeed hard to find programs and practices that don't work. As described in *Visible Learning* (Hattie, 2009), we have to reject the starting point of zero. Students naturally mature and develop over the course of a year, and thus actions, activities, and interventions that teachers use should *extend learning beyond what a student can achieve by simply attending school for a year.*

This is why John Hattie set the bar of acceptability higher—at the average of all the influences he compiled—from the home, parents, schools, teachers, curricula, and teaching strategies. This average was 0.40, and Hattie called it the "hinge point." He then undertook to study the underlying attributes that would explain why those influences higher than 0.40 had such a positive impact compared with those lower than 0.40. His findings were the impetus for the *Visible Learning* story.

Borrowing from *Visible Learning*, the barometer and hinge point are effective in explaining what we focus on in this book and why. Here's an example of how this might play out from literacy:

Let's focus on sentence-combining efforts, which are popular in literacy education circles. In essence, students are taught to use punctuation, compound sentences, subordination, reduction, and apposition to take two or more sentences and produce one. For example, students might be given the following three sentences and asked to combine them:

John F. Kennedy was inaugurated into office in January 1961.

He was assassinated in November 1963.

He spent only 1,000 days in office.

There are a number of correct responses to this task, but students may incorrectly think that the combined sentences are better, that sentence complexity is important above all else, or that combined sentences maintain the same meaning and focus as uncombined sentences. But as with much of the educational research, there are studies that contradict other studies. For example, Wilkinson and Patty (1993) compared sentence-combining instruction with a placebo treatment and found significantly better results for sentence combining. But did their sentence-combining approach raise achievement over that which was expected from simply attending school for a year? That's where the meta-analyses and effect size efforts can teach us. The barometer and hinge point for sentence combining are presented in Figure 1.2. Note that this approach rests in the zone of "developmental effects," which is below the teacher effects and better than reverse effects.

THE BAROMETER FOR THE INFLUENCE OF SENTENCE COMBINING

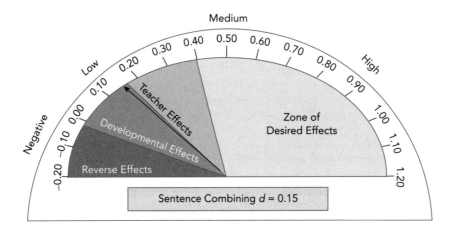

Source: Adapted from Hattie (2012).

Figure 1.2

Our focus in *Visible Learning for Literacy* is on actions that fall inside the *zone of desired effects*, which is 0.40 and above. When actions are in the range of 0.40 and above, the data suggest that the learning extends beyond that which was expected from attending school for a year.

Caution: That doesn't mean that everything below 0.40 effect size is not worthy of attention. In fact, there are likely some useful approaches for teaching and learning that are not above this average. For example, drama and arts programs have an effect size of 0.35, almost ensuring that students gain a year's worth of achievement for a year of education. We are not suggesting that drama and art be removed from the curriculum. In fact, artistic expression and aesthetic understanding may be valuable in and of themselves. Another critical finding was the very low effect of teacher's subject matter knowledge. While we may accept the evidence that it is currently of little import, surely this means we should worry considerably and investigate, first, why it is so

EFFECT SIZE
FOR DRAMA/ARTS
PROGRAMS = 0.35

low and, second, how we can change what we do in the classroom to ensure that the knowledge teachers bring to the classroom has a much higher effect.

It is important to note that some of the aggregate scores mask situations in which specific actions can be strategically used to improve students' understanding. Simulations are a good case. The effect size for simulations is 0.33, below the threshold that we established. But, what if simulations were really effective in deepening understanding but really, really bad when used with surface learning? In this case, the strategic deployment of simulations could be important. There are situations like this that we will review in this book as we focus on surface-level literacy learning versus deep literacy learning and transfer learning. For now, let's turn our attention to actions that teachers can take to improve student learning.

EFFECT SIZE FOR SIMULATIONS = **0.33**

Learning From What Works, Not Limited to Literacy

The majority of this book will focus on literacy, specifically. In this next section, however, we focus our attention more broadly. Literacy instruction is situated in a larger classroom environment, and learning to read, write, speak, listen, and view is contextualized in the general learning situations that students encounter. We believe that the following influences deserve attention from teachers in all classes, including those devoted to literacy.

Teacher Credibility

A few things come to mind when we consider actions that teachers can take at the more generic level. On the top of the list, with an effect size of 0.90, is teacher credibility. Students know which teachers can make a difference in their lives. Teacher credibility is a constellation of characteristics, including trust, competence, dynamism, and immediacy. Students evaluate each of these factors to determine if their teacher is credible, and if they are going to choose to learn

EFFECT SIZE FOR TEACHER CREDIBILITY = **0.90**

from that teacher. Teachers can compromise their credibility when they violate trust, make a lot of errors, sit in the back of the room, or lack a sense of urgency. They compromise their credibility particularly if they are not seen to be fair. Of course, each of these needs to be held in balance. For example, too much pressure, and students will think that a given teacher is a stress case. Not enough, and they'll think their teacher doesn't care. Similarly, students might think a teacher is weird when he or she fakes excitement about a topic of study, or realize that their teacher doesn't care about the unit at all. Although not specifically focused on literacy, the dynamic of teacher credibility is always at play.

Consider Angela Conner. She's always excited about everything. She knows her content well and works to establish trusting relationships with her students. But every time something happens, it's as if it's the most important and exciting thing ever. She is over the top with enthusiasm. This worked well for her with her kindergarten students, but her fifth graders think she's a fake. As one of the students said, "Yeah, Ms. Conner pretends to be excited, even when we get a test back. Really? It's important, but it's not like she should be jumping around like she does." This student, and likely many more, is questioning Ms. Conner's credibility and thus compromising her students' ability to learn from her.

On the other hand, Brandon Chu exudes excitement episodically, and his students wait for it. Things seem very important to Mr. Chu, and he tells his students why things are important and how the class builds on itself over the course of the year. In one lesson, Mr. Chu said, "We've got some pressure on us to get some major work done. It's crunch time, people, and we need to support each other in our learning. Please make sure that each of you has completed the concept map and are ready to write. If you haven't had a peer review yet, let me know. We need to get these done so that they can be included in the upcoming e-zine. If we miss the deadline, we're out of the issue." Mr. Chu's students trust him and know when it's time to focus. They appreciate his dynamic yet not overzealous style. And, parenthetically, they learn a lot.

Our focus is on actions that fall inside the *zone of desired effects*. When actions are in this range, the data suggest that the effort extends beyond that which was expected from attending school for a year.

EFFECT SIZE FOR CONCEPT MAPPING = 0.60

Teacher–Student Relationships

Closely related to teacher credibility is teacher–student relationships, which have an effect size of 0.72. When students believe that the teacher is credible, they are more likely to develop positive relationships with that teacher, and then learn more from him or her. But relationships go deeper than credibility. Of course, relationships are based on trust, which is part of the credibility construct. But relationships also require effective communication and addressing issues that strain the relationship. Positive relationships are fostered and maintained when teachers set fair expectations, involve students in determining aspects of the classroom organization and management, and hold students accountable for the expectations in an equitable way. Importantly, relationships are not destroyed when problematic behaviors occur, on the part of either the teacher or students. This is an important point for literacy educators. If we want to ensure students read, write, communicate, and think at high levels, we have to develop positive, trusting relationships with students, all students.

EFFECT SIZE FOR
TEACHER–STUDENT
RELATIONSHIPS
= 0.72

The optimal relationships also include when the teacher establishes high levels of trust among the students. When students ask a question indicating they are lost, do not know where they are going, or are just plain wrong, high levels of peer-to-peer trust means that these students are not ridiculed, do not feel that they should be silent and bear their not knowing, and can depend on the teacher and often other students to help them out.

Unfortunately, in some cases, specific students are targeted for behavioral correction while other students engaged in the same behavior are not noticed. This happens often across the K–12 grade span. We remember a primary-grade classroom in which a student with a disability was repeatedly chastised for a problematic behavior, but other children engaged in the same behavior were ignored and allowed to continue. Yes, the children noticed. As one of the students said, "Mr. Henderson doesn't want Michael in our class." It's hard to develop positive relationships, and then achieve, when you are not wanted. But, perhaps even more importantly, the poor relationship between Mr. Henderson and

Video 1.1
Teacher–Student
Relationships That
Impact Learning

*http://resources.corwin.com/
VL-Literacy*

*To read a QR code, you must
have a smartphone or tablet with
a camera. We recommend that you
download a QR code reader app
that is made specifically for your
phone or tablet brand.*

Michael spilled over to the rest of the students who didn't think their teacher was fair or that he was trustworthy.

We have also observed this phenomenon in secondary classrooms. There always seem to be some students who can get away with problematic behavior. Sometimes, these students are athletes; other times, they're cheerleaders or drama students or musicians or students whose parents work in the district. It doesn't really matter which group they belong to; their status allows them to get away with things that other students don't. And it always compromises the trust students have with their teacher and the relationships that develop.

But we're not saying that literacy educators should be strict disciplinarians who mete out punishments and consequences for every infraction. We are saying that it's important to be consistent, to be fair, and to repair relationships that are damaged when problematic behavior occurs. To develop positive relationships, it's important that teachers

- Display student work

- Share class achievements

- Speak to the accomplishments of all students

- Be sincere in their pride in their students and make sure that pride is based on evidence of student work, not generalized comments

- Look for opportunities for students to be proud of themselves and of other students or groups of students

- Develop parental pride in student accomplishments

- Develop pride in improvement in addition to pride in excellence

As we mentioned above, teachers also have the responsibility to repair harm to relationships. These restorative practices allow students to take responsibility for their behavior and to make amends. This can be a simple impromptu conference, a class meeting or circle, or a more formal victim–offender dialogue. Regardless, the point is to ensure that students understand that their actions caused harm and that they can repair that harm. Figure 1.3 contains questions, developed by the International

RESTORATIVE CONFERENCING

Questions to Ask the Offender	Questions to Ask the Victim
• "What happened?" • "What were you thinking about at the time?" • "What have you thought about since the incident?" • "Who do you think has been affected by your actions?" • "How have they been affected?"	• "What was your reaction at the time of the incident?" • "How do you feel about what happened?" • "What has been the hardest thing for you?" • "How did your family and friends react when they heard about the incident?"

Source: Restorative Conference Facilitator Script, Restorative Conferencing, International Institute on Restorative Practices, http://www.iirp.edu/article_detail.php?article_id=NjYy

Figure 1.3

Institute for Restorative Practices, that allow people to figure out what went wrong and how to repair the harm that has been done. We've spent time on this because relationships matter, and students achieve more and better when they develop strong interpersonal relationships with their teachers. It's these humane and growth-producing conversations that help students grow in their prosocial behaviors. (Note that the greatest effect on achievement when students join a new class or school is related to whether they make a friend in the first month— it is your job to worry about friendship, counter loneliness, and help students gain a reputation as great learners not only in your eyes but also in the eyes of their peers.) And by the way, effectively managed classrooms, ones in which students understand the expectations and are held to those expectations in ways that are consistent with relationship development and maintenance, have an effect size of 0.52. A poorly run classroom will interfere with high-quality literacy learning.

EFFECT SIZE FOR CLASSROOM MANAGEMENT = 0.52

Teacher Expectations

Another influence on student achievement that is important for literacy educators, but isn't directly a literacy approach, is teacher expectations,

EFFECT SIZE FOR
EXPECTATIONS = 0.43

with an effect size of 0.43. In large part, teachers get what they expect; yes, teachers with low expectations are particularly successful at getting what they expect. The more recent research has shown that teachers who have high (or low) expectations tend to have them for all their students (Rubie-Davies, 2015). Teachers' expectations of students become the reality for students. Requiring kindergarteners to master 100 sight words, and then aligning instruction to accomplish that, communicates the expectations a teacher has for five-year-olds. Believing that ninth graders can only write five-paragraph essays with 500 words sets the bar very low, and students will jump just that high, and no higher than that. Over time, students exert just enough effort to meet teacher expectations. Hattie (2012) called this the *minimax* principle, "maximum grade return for minimal extra effort" (p. 93). And it gets in the way of better and deeper learning. When expectations are high, the minimax principle can work to facilitate students' learning.

This does not mean that teachers should set unrealistic expectations. Telling first graders that they are required to read Tolstoy's *War and Peace* is a bit too far. Teachers should have expectations that appropriately stretch students, and yet those expectations should be within reach. Sixth graders who are held to fourth-grade expectations will be great fifth graders when they are in seventh grade; the gap never closes. And students deserve more. When high-yield literacy instructional routines are utilized, students can achieve more than a year's growth during a year of instruction. And that's what this book focuses on—maximizing the impact teachers have on students' learning.

Establishing and communicating a learning intention is an important way that teachers share their expectations with students. When these learning intentions are compared with grade-level expectations, or expectations in other schools and districts, educators can get a sense of their appropriateness. We will spend a lot more time later in this book focused on learning intentions and success criteria. Another way to assess the level of expectation is to invite students to share their goals for learning with their teachers—especially early in the instructional sequence. If students have low expectations for themselves, they're likely hearing that from the adults around them, and often this is what they achieve. And finally, analyzing the success criteria is an important way of determining the expectations a teacher has for students. A given learning intention could have multiple success criteria, some of which may be fairly low and others of which may be high. The success criteria communicate the level of performance that students are expected to meet, yet are often overlooked in explorations about teacher expectations. We'll return to success criteria in the next section of this chapter, but before we do so, it's important to note that teachers establish expectations in other ways beyond the learning intention.

The ways in which teachers consciously and subconsciously communicate their expectations to students are too numerous to list. Expectations are everywhere, in every exchange teachers and students have. When teachers use academic language in their interactions with others, they communicate their expectations. When teachers maintain a clean and inviting classroom, they communicate their expectations. When teachers assign mindless shut-up sheets, they communicate their expectations. When teachers provide honest feedback about students' work, they communicate their expectations. When teachers give one class two days to complete work and another class one day, they communicate their expectations. We could go on. Students watch their teachers all the time trying to figure out what is expected of them and if they are trustworthy. Literacy learning can be enhanced when teachers communicate specific, relevant, and appropriate expectations for students. From there, teachers can design amazing learning environments. But it's more than instruction. Teachers should focus on *learning*. It's a mindset that we all need, if we are going to ensure that students develop their literate selves. A major theme throughout this book is how teachers think (and also how we want students to think). Hattie (2012) suggests 10 mind frames that can be used to guide decisions, from curriculum adoptions to lesson planning (Figure 1.4).

Taken together, these mind frames summarize a great deal of the "what works" literature. In the remainder of this book, we focus on putting these into practice specifically as they relate to literacy learning, and address the better question, *what works best?* (Hattie, 2009). To do so, we need to consider the levels of learning we can expect from students. How,

Video 1.2
Making Learning Visible With Teacher Clarity and Expectations

http://resources.corwin.com/ VL-Literacy

EFFECT SIZE FOR TEACHER CLARITY = 0.75

MIND FRAMES FOR TEACHERS

1. I cooperate with other teachers.

2. I use dialogue, not monologue.

3. I set the challenge.

4. I talk about learning, not teaching.

5. I inform all about the language of learning.

6. I see learning as hard work.

7. Assessment is feedback to me about me.

8. I am a change agent.

9. I am an evaluator.

10. I develop positive relationships.

Source: Hattie (2012). Reproduced with permission.

Figure 1.4

then, should we define learning, since that is our goal? As John himself suggested in his 2014 Vernon Wall Lecture, learning can be defined as

> [t]he process of developing sufficient surface knowledge to then move to deeper understanding such that one can appropriately transfer this learning to new tasks and situations.

Learning is a process, not an event. And there is a scale for learning. Some things students only understand at the surface level. As we note in the next chapter, surface learning is not valued, but it should be. You have to know something to be able to do something with it. We've never met a student who could synthesize information from multiple sources who didn't have an understanding of each of the texts. With appropriate instruction about how to relate and extend ideas, surface learning becomes deep understanding. Deep understanding is important if students are going to set their own expectations and monitor their own achievement. But schooling should not stop there. Learning demands that students be able to apply—transfer—their knowledge, skills, and strategies to new tasks and new situations. That transfer is so difficult to attain is one of our closely kept secrets—so often we pronounce that students can transfer, but the process of teaching them this skill is too often not discussed. We will discuss it in Chapter 4.

EFFECT SIZE FOR SELF-REPORTED GRADES/STUDENT EXPECTATIONS = **1.44**

Unfortunately, up to 90% of the instruction we conduct can be completed by students using *only* the surface-level skills (Hattie, 2012). Read that sentence carefully—it did not say that teachers do not ask students to complete deeper analyses, and it did not say that teachers do not ask students to complete tests and assignments that focus on deeper learning. It said that students only need a high level of surface-level knowledge to do well on this work. Why? Because teachers value surface learning while often preaching deeper learning. We need to balance our expectations with our reality. This means more constructive alignment between what teachers claim success looks like, how the tasks students are assigned align with these claims about success, and how success is measured by end-of-course assessments or assignments. It is not a matter of all surface or all deep; it is a matter of being clear when surface and when deep is truly required.

The ultimate goal, and one that is hard to realize, is transfer (see Figure 1.5 on the next page). When students reach this level, learning has been accomplished. One challenge to this model is that most assessments focus on surface-level learning because that level is easier to evaluate. But, as David Coleman, president of the College Board, said in his Los Angeles Unified presentation to administrators, test makers have to assume responsibility for the practice their assessment inspires. That applies to all of us. If the assessment focuses on recall, then a great number of instructional minutes will be devoted to developing students' ability to demonstrate "learning" that way.

As teachers, we are faced with a wide range of assessments used to evaluate student achievement and teacher performance. But these come and go. Teachers also make tests and should assume responsibility for the practices that result from their own creations.

LEARNING DEFINED: THE THREE-PHASE MODEL

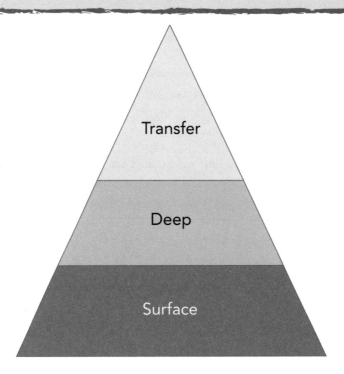

Figure 1.5

During an English department meeting at our school in San Diego, a group of teachers proposed a cumulative final exam. One of them said, "It would be better to mirror the expectations in college if we used a final exam as part of our grades."

As the discussion continued, another teacher asked, "How many days do you think we'll spend reviewing for the final?"

The range of answers was one day to two weeks. The assessment would change practice. Another said, "What about building transfer tasks for students to complete so that they would know that they had mastered the content for our courses? If we asked them to apply their knowledge to new tasks, we'd know they learned it, right? And we wouldn't spend hours reviewing the past."

The conversation continued, and this group of teachers made their decision. Our point here is not to debate the merits of final exams, but rather to focus on the levels of learning and the fact that teachers can choose to engage students in deeper understanding. It's within our power, as the mind frames suggest, to do so.

In this book, we devote time to each level or phase of learning. Importantly, there are teacher and student actions that work best at each of these phases. For example, note-taking works well for surface-level learning whereas repeated reading and close reading probably work better for deep learning. A key point that we will make repeatedly is that teachers have to understand the impact that they have on students, and choose approaches that will maximize that impact. Mismatching an approach with the level of learning expected will not create the desired impact. *What* and *when* are equally important when it comes to instruction that has an impact on learning.

> *What* and *when* are equally important when it comes to instruction that has an impact on learning.

General Literacy Learning Practices

Before we dive into the levels of learning as they relate to literacy, there are three aspects of learning that transcend the three-phase model:

1. Challenge

2. Self-efficacy

3. Learning intentions with success criteria

These should be considered in each and every learning situation as they are global factors that impact understanding. We explain each of these in more detail below.

1. Challenge

The first of these global aspects is challenge. Students appreciate challenge. They expect to work hard to achieve success in school and life. When tasks become too easy, students get bored. Similarly, when tasks become too difficult, students get frustrated. There is a sweet spot for learning, but the problem is that it differs for different students. There is a Goldilocks notion of making a task not too easy or too hard but just right. As Tomlinson (2005) noted,

> Ensuring challenge is calibrated to the particular needs of a learner at a particular time is one of the most essential roles of the teacher and appears non-negotiable for student growth. Our best understanding suggests that a student only learns when work is moderately challenging that student, and where there is assistance to help the student master what initially seems out of reach. (pp. 163–164)

How, then, can literacy educators keep students challenged but not frustrated? There are several responses to this question, and our answer is embedded in every chapter of this book. In part, we would respond that the type of learning intention is important to maintain challenge.

Learning Intention: Surface, Deep, or Transfer

The teacher should know if students need surface-, deep-, or transfer-type work—or what combination—while ensuring the parts are explicit for the student. In this way, the teacher can maintain the challenge while providing appropriate instructional supports. Showing students near the beginning of a series of lessons what success at the end should look like is among the more powerful things we can do to enhance learning. There are many ways to do this—among them,

- Showing them worked examples of an A, B, and C piece of work, and discussing how they differ
- Giving them the scoring rubrics at the outset and teaching them what they mean
- Sharing last year's students' work in the same series of lessons
- Building a concept map with them up front to show the interrelationships between the various parts they will learn about

—anything to help provide a coat hanger for students to know what good enough is, what success looks like, how they will know when they get there. Not showing this is like asking a high jumper to jump the bar but not telling or showing him or her how high the bar is!

Student-to-Student Interaction

In addition, we would note that schools should be filled with student-to-student interaction. As one of the mind frames above suggests, classrooms should be filled with dialogue rather than monologues. We say this for several reasons, including the fact that no one gets good at something he or she doesn't do. If students aren't using language— speaking, listening, reading, and writing—they're not likely to excel in those areas. Further, as students work collaboratively and cooperatively, the assigned tasks can be more complex because there are many minds at work on solving the tasks. Of course, this requires clear expectations for group work and instruction about how to work with others. But the outcomes are worth it—students learn more deeply when they are engaged in complex tasks that involve collaboration (they don't necessarily learn more from collaborating with others when the learning focuses on surface-level content). Further, when students work together in groups, they have an opportunity to engage in peer tutoring, which has an effect size of 0.55.

> EFFECT SIZE FOR COOPERATIVE LEARNING = **0.42**

> EFFECT SIZE FOR PEER TUTORING = **0.55**

Feedback

How else can we maintain challenge for each learner? Our third response relates to feedback. When students are engaged in appropriately challenging tasks, they are more likely to respond to feedback because they need that information to continue growing and learning. Feedback focused on something that you already know does little to change understanding. Feedback thrives on errors. For example, Marco has a strong sense of English spelling. His writing is filled with complex vocabulary terms that are spelled correctly. He understands how to use resources to build this knowledge about words. Thus, feedback about the misspelling of the word *acknowledge*, which he spelled "acknowlege" in his handwritten draft, is not likely to result in great changes in his learning. Any spell-check program on a computer will tell him he is wrong, and he can correct it. A better use of time might be to focus on Marco's use of clichés in his writing. A useful conversation with him could show him that the more familiar a term or phrase becomes, the more often readers skip over it as they read, essentially rendering the text ineffective.

What Makes a Task Challenging?

Unfortunately, some people confuse difficulty with complexity. We like to think of *difficulty* as the amount of effort or work a student is expected to put forth whereas *complexity* is the level of thinking, the number of steps, or the abstractness of the task. We don't believe that teachers can radically impact students' learning by making them do a lot more work. We know that students learn more when they are engaged in deeper thinking. That's not to say that difficulty is bad. We think of this in four quadrants (see Figure 1.6). The quadrant that includes low difficulty and low complexity is not unimportant. We think that note-taking fits into that quadrant. If that's all students experience, learning isn't likely to be robust. However, learning to take notes, and then engaging in study skills with those notes (which likely raises the complexity but not the difficulty), could impact learning. As part of each lesson, teachers should know the level of difficulty and complexity they are requiring of students. They can then make decisions about differentiation and instructional support, as well as feedback that will move learning forward.

> We don't believe that teachers can radically impact students' learning by making them do a lot more work.

2. Self-Efficacy

A second global consideration for literacy educators is students' self-efficacy. Hattie (2012) defines self-efficacy as "the confidence or strength of belief that we have in ourselves that we can make our learning happen" (p. 45). He continues, with descriptions of students with high self-efficacy, noting that they

- Understand complex tasks as challenges rather than trying to avoid them

- Experience failure as opportunities to learn, which may require additional effort, information, support, time, and so on

- Quickly recover a sense of confidence after setbacks

By contrast, students with low self-efficacy

- Avoid complex and difficult tasks (as these are seen as personal threats)

DIFFICULTY AND COMPLEXITY

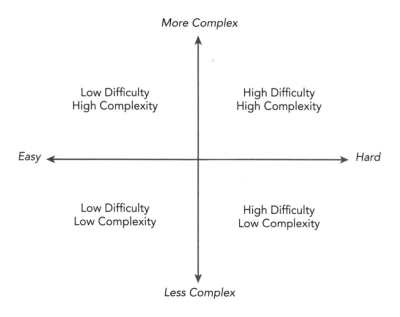

More Complex

Low Difficulty
High Complexity

High Difficulty
High Complexity

Easy ← → Hard

Low Difficulty
Low Complexity

High Difficulty
Low Complexity

Less Complex

Figure 1.6

- Maintain weak commitment to goals

- Experience failure as a personal deficiency

- Slowly recover a sense of confidence after setbacks

It almost goes without saying that the impact of self-efficacy on learning is significant. Our emotions, the sense of failure, and our anxieties are often invoked in our learning—or more often in our resistance to engage in learning. Building a sense of confidence that you can indeed attain the criteria of success for the lessons may be a first critical step—without a sense of confidence, we often do not open our ears to what we are being taught. Most of us are more likely to engage in difficult, complex, or risky learning if we know there is help nearby, that there are safety nets, that we will not be ridiculed if we do not succeed—this is where the power of the teacher lies.

Students with high self-efficacy perform better and understand that their efforts can result in better learning. This becomes a self-fulfilling prophecy: the rich get richer, and the poor get poorer. Students with poor self-efficacy see each challenge and setback as evidence that they aren't learning, and in fact can't learn, which reduces the likelihood that they will rally the forces for the next task the teacher assigns.

In their study about ways to increase students' self-efficacy, Mathisen and Bronnick (2009) suggested a combination of the following (each of which is addressed later in this book in more detail):

- Direct instruction with modeled examples

- Verbal persuasion through introductory information

- Feedback on attempts made by learners

- Guided use of techniques on well-defined problems

- Supervised use of techniques on self-generated problems

To this we add

- Demonstrating your credibility by being fair to all

- Being there to help students reach targets

- Creating high levels of trust between yourself and the students and between students

- Showing that you welcome errors as opportunities for learning

Others have made different recommendations (e.g., Linnenbrink & Pintrich, 2003), and our point here is not to endorse one approach over another but rather to confirm that teachers can change students' agency and identity such that self-efficacy, the "belief that we have in ourselves that we can make our learning happen" (Hattie, 2012, p. 46), is fostered.

3. Learning Intentions With Success Criteria

The third and final global aspect that should permeate literacy learning relates to being explicit about the nature of learning that students are expected to do and the level of success expected from the lesson. Teacher clarity about learning expectations, including the ways in which students can demonstrate their understanding, is powerful. The effect size is 0.75. Every lesson, irrespective of whether it focuses on surface, deep, or transfer, needs to have clearly articulated learning intention and success criteria. We believe that students should be able to answer, and ask, these questions of each lesson:

EFFECT SIZE
FOR TEACHER
CLARITY = **0.75**

1. What am I learning today?

2. Why am I learning this?

3. How will I know that I learned it?

The first question requires deep understanding of the learning intention. The second question begs for relevance, and the third question focuses on the success criteria. Neglecting any of these questions compromises students' learning. In fact, we argue that these questions compose part of the Learner's Bill of Rights. Given that teachers (and the public at large) judge students based on their performance, it seems only fair that students should know what they are expected to learn, why they are learning that, and how success will be determined. The marks teachers make on report cards and transcripts become part of the permanent record that follows students around. Those documents have the power to change parents' perceptions of their child, determine future placements in school, and open college doors. And it works. Clearly articulating the goals for learning has an effect size of 0.50. It's the right thing to do, and it's effective.

EFFECT SIZE FOR
GOALS = **0.50**

We're not saying that it's easy to identify learning intentions and success criteria. Smith (2007) notes, "Writing learning intentions and success criteria is not easy . . . because it forces us to 'really, really think' about what we want the pupils to learn rather than simply accepting statements handed on by others" (p. 14). We are saying that it's worth the effort.

Learning intentions are more than a standard. There have been far too many misguided efforts that mandated teachers to post the standard on the wall. Learning intentions are based on the standard, but are chunked into learning bites. In too many cases, the standards are not understandable to students. Learning intentions, if they are to be effective,

Video 1.3
Making Learning
Visible Through
Learning Intentions

*http://resources.corwin.com/
VL-Literacy*

have to be understood and accepted by students. Simply writing a target on the dry-erase board and then reading it aloud waters down the power of a learning intention, which should focus the entire lesson and serve as an organizing feature of the learning students do. At minimum, learning intentions should bookend lessons with clear communication about the learning target. In addition, teachers can remind students of the learning intention at each transition point throughout the lesson. In this way, the learning intention drives the lesson, and students will develop a better understanding of how close they are to mastering the expectations. Most critical, the learning intention should demonstrably lead to the criteria of success—and if you had to use only one of these, we would recommend focusing on being more explicit about the success criteria. Both help, but the judgment about the standard of work desired is more important than explication about the particular tasks we ask students to do. It is the height of the bar, not the bar, that matters.

Figure 1.7 contains some poorly written learning intentions and some improvements that teachers made collaboratively as they explored the value of this approach. Note that the intentions became longer, more specific, and more interesting. The improved versions invite students into learning. Of course, learning intentions can be grouped. Sometimes an activity can contribute to several learning intentions, and other times a learning intention requires several activities. However, when learning intentions spread over many days, student interest will wane, and motivation will decrease. When teachers plan a unit of study and clearly identify the learning intentions required for mastery of the content, most times they can identify daily targets. In doing so, they can also identify the success criteria, which will allow for checking for understanding and targeted feedback.

The success criteria must be directly linked with learning intentions to have any impact. The success criteria describe how students will be expected to demonstrate their learning, based on the learning intention. That's not to say that success criteria are just a culminating activity, but they can be. Consider the following ways that students might demonstrate success based on a learning intention that reads, "Analyze visual images presented in the text and determine how this information contributes to and clarifies information."

SAMPLE LEARNING INTENTIONS

Grade	Poor Example	Improved Version
K	Compare the experiences of characters in two stories.	Today, we'll read two stories about city and country life. We'll focus on comparing the lives of the two characters and the differences in their lives based on where they live.
5	Use technical language in the revisions of essays.	As we revise our opinion papers, we are going to learn how to update our word choices so that we use technical vocabulary like the authors we've been studying use.
7	Determine the central idea of a text.	Each group has a different article, and our learning today is going to focus on locating the central or controlling idea, the idea that the author uses to hold the entire text together.
11	Compare two texts for different themes.	Compare how two texts from the same point in U.S. history address a common theme and figure out what each author is trying to say in response to the theme.

Figure 1.7

- Discuss with a partner the way the author used visuals and how they helped you understand the text.

- Identify one place in the text that was confusing and how one of the visuals helped you understand that information.

- In your annotations, make sure to include situations where the visual information helped you understand the text itself.

- Create a visual that will help another person understand the words in the text.

All of these work, in different situations. Clarity is important here. What is it that students should be learning, and how will they know (not to mention how will the teacher know) if they learned it? That's the power of learning intentions and success criteria.

Importantly, students can be involved in establishing the success criteria and, in many cases, the learning intentions. Teachers can ask their

Video 1.4

Making Success Criteria
Visible in Fourth Grade

*http://resources.corwin.com/
VL-Literacy*

EFFECT SIZE
FOR PEER
TUTORING = **0.55**

EFFECT SIZE FOR
COOPERATIVE
VERSUS
COMPETITIVE
LEARNING = **0.54**

EFFECT SIZE
FOR STUDENT-
CENTERED
TEACHING = **0.54**

students, "How will you know you have learned this? What evidence could we accept that learning has occurred?" In these situations, students can share their thinking about the success criteria, and often they are more demanding of themselves than their teachers are. In a sixth-grade English class focused on learning to come to group discussions prepared, the students identified several ways that they would know if they met this expectation. Several suggested that they should have their learning materials with them when they moved into collaborative learning. Others added that they should have their notes and annotations updated and be ready to talk about their reading, rather than read while they are in the group. One student suggested that they should practice vocabulary before the group so that they would be ready. Another added that they should each know their role in the group so that they can get started right away. None of these answers were wrong; they were all useful in improving the collaborative learning time. In this case, the students established the success criteria and opened the door to feedback from their peers and the teacher in their successive approximations in demonstrating mastery of their learning.

Further, when students understand the success criteria, they can be most involved in assessing their own success, and their progression toward this success. A simple tool allows students to put sticky notes in one of four quadrants to communicate their status (see Figure 1.8). This alerts the teacher, and other students, about help that is needed. It mobilizes peer tutoring and cooperative versus competitive learning, as well as building student-centered teaching.

Other times, the tools used to create the success criteria involve rubrics and checklists. For example, students in a high school language arts class were tasked with selecting a worthy cause, something that they cared passionately about and whose value they could explain to others. Students were encouraged to select topics that were personally relevant and to learn more about that topic. As part of the assignment, students wrote an analytic essay about their chosen topic. Another part of the project required that they develop a web page, a Facebook page, or another electronic way of communicating with a wider world about their cause. And still another part of their assignment required the development of an informational pamphlet that they could use to educate adults about the

SAMPLE SELF-ASSESSMENT OF LEARNING

I do not **yet** understand. I need coaching.	I am starting to understand. I need coaching but want to try some on my own.
I understand! I make a few mistakes, so I'm working through those.	I understand **very** well. I can explain this to others without telling them the answers.

Figure 1.8

 Template available for download at **http://resources.corwin.com/VL-Literacy**

issue. Students selected a range of worthy causes, from Islamophobia to endangered animals to mental health. Figure 1.9 on the next page contains the checklist that the teachers used to communicate their expectations to students. Note that many of these are compliance-related items that will subsequently allow teachers, and students, to determine if the experience left a lasting impact. The teachers were aiming to tap into and integrated curricular approaches. They were also looking for evidence of learning transfer, asking students to mobilize their literacy skills for a task they had not completed before.

Clearly articulating the success criteria allows errors to become more obvious. Errors should be expected and celebrated because they are opportunities for learning. If students are not making errors, they have likely previously mastered the learning intention. Also note that feedback thrives on the presence of errors. Errors should be the hallmark of learning—if we are not making enough errors, we are not stretching ourselves; if we make too many, we need more help to start in a different place. Unfortunately, in too many classrooms, students who already know the content are privileged, and students who make errors feel shame. In those situations, learning isn't occurring for students who already know the content; they've already learned it. But learning isn't occurring for the students who make errors because they hide their errors and avoid feedback. Classrooms have to be safe places for errors to be recognized.

EFFECT SIZE
FOR CREATIVITY
PROGRAMS ON
ACHIEVEMENT = **0.65**

EFFECT SIZE
FOR INTEGRATED
CURRICULA
PROGRAMS = **0.39**

SAMPLE PROJECT CHECKLIST

Pamphlet Portion		
Item	Date Projected	Completed ✓
Cover has the title, image, and your name		
Description of your cause (minimum 10 sentences)		
List 3–5 important facts		
Map of where this is occurring		
Demographics of who/what is impacted		
Minimum of 3 images in your brochure		
Contact information (websites, telephone numbers)		
Upcoming events (celebrations, day, movie, anniversary date, races, etc.)		
Pamphlet is attractive and well organized		
Correct spelling and grammar		

Figure 1.9

 Template available for download at **http://resources.corwin.com/VL-Literacy**

For example, a secondary science class was focused on reviewing the changes in climate—there were clipboards everywhere, with students running around the school checking temperatures. They had great analyses and stunning box and whisker plots. But when they were asked how long they had been doing this task, they said three weeks (and that it was fun). What a waste. Perfection is not necessarily the aim of lessons; the presence of errors is a better indicator of a successful lesson, and surely hints to the teacher and student where is the most likely place to go next.

When errors are celebrated and expected, feedback takes hold. Feedback has a powerful impact on student learning, with an effect size of 0.75, placing it in the top 10 influences on achievement. But it's only when the feedback is received that it works. Giving feedback is different from receiving feedback. Feedback is designed to close the gap between students' current level of understanding or performance and the expected level of performance, which we call the success criteria. For feedback to work, teachers have to understand

- Students' current level of performance

- Students' expected level of performance

- Actions they can take to close the gap

Feedback, as Brookhart (2008) describes it, needs to be "just-in-time, just-for-me information delivered when and where it can do the most good" (p. 1). Figure 1.10 on the next page includes information about the ways in which feedback can vary in terms of timing, amount, mode, and audience. We'll focus on feedback in greater depth in the chapter on deep literacy learning (Chapter 3). For now, we hope you appreciate the value of feedback in impacting student learning.

> EFFECT SIZE FOR
> FEEDBACK = 0.75

Conclusion

Teachers, we have choices. We can elect to use instructional routines and procedures that don't work, or that don't work for the intended purpose. Or we can embrace the evidence, update our classrooms, and impact student learning in wildly positive ways. We can choose to move beyond surface-level learning, while still honoring the importance of teaching students surface-level skills and strategies. We can extend students' learning in deep ways and facilitate the transfer of their learning to new tasks, texts, and projects, if we want. We can design amazing lessons that mobilize the evidence and provide opportunities for students to learn. And we can decide to evaluate our impact, if we are brave enough.

Monica was lucky enough to transfer to a school that embraced *Visible Learning for Literacy*. Her teachers tried out the instructional ideas, monitored progress, and provided feedback to her and to each other. Monica went from a failing student, tracked in a class with low expectations, to a lead learner providing support for her peers. Impact has a face. It's not an abstract idea or ideal. Together, we can impact the literacy learning of every student. Let's make it so.

> Errors should be expected and celebrated because they are opportunities for learning. If students are not making errors, they have likely previously mastered the learning intention.

FEEDBACK STRATEGIES

Feedback Strategies Can Vary in . . .	In These Ways . . .	Recommendations for Good Feedback
Timing	• When given • How often	• Provide immediate feedback for knowledge of facts (right/wrong). • Delay feedback slightly for more comprehensive reviews of student thinking and processing. • Never delay feedback beyond when it would make a difference to students. • Provide feedback as often as is practical, for all major assignments.
Amount	• How many points made • How much about each point	• Prioritize—pick the most important points. • Choose points that relate to major learning goals. • Consider the student's developmental level.
Mode	• Oral • Written • Visual/ demonstration	• Select the best mode for the message. Would a comment in passing the student's desk suffice? Is a conference needed? • Interactive feedback (talking with the student) is best when possible. • Give written feedback on written work or on assignment cover sheets. • Use demonstration if "how to do something" is an issue or if the student needs an example.
Audience	• Individual • Group/class	• Individual feedback says, "The teacher values my learning." • Group/class feedback works if most of the class missed the same concept on an assignment, which presents an opportunity for reteaching.

Source: Brookhart (2008).

Figure 1.10

SURFACE LITERACY LEARNING

2

The phrase "surface learning" holds a negative connotation for many people. Teachers are hesitant to acknowledge that anything they do is at the surface level, but to say so is to dismiss the essential practice of a strong start. Consider the deep wells of knowledge and skills you possess about your professional practice. Now recall how it began. In all likelihood, it began formally in your teacher preparation program, but it certainly didn't stop there. Over time, you have been able to craft that initial knowledge into a broader and deeper set of practices that allow you to respond effectively to new and novel situations. It is about getting the balance between these three right, not one or the others. Skilled teachers know, for example, that their students and the context shift each year. Teaching the same grade level or content for multiple years does not mean that the instruction is static. Quite the opposite: skilled teaching is dynamic teaching.

But it all begins somewhere. Like a swimmer entering the water, the initial steps require breaking the surface. Nothing else can occur if the entry never happens. As well, a strong beginning sets the stage for later success. A student isn't going to be able to evaluate two pieces of contradictory texts if she doesn't have a solid grounding in what each of the texts means at the literal, structural, and inferential levels. In other words, a reader's ability to engage in interpretive and critical thinking can be inhibited if she hasn't had the opportunity to acquire and consolidate the knowledge and skills she will need. You need surface learning to be able to relate, extend, and think deeply. It is a matter of proportion—when you first are exposed to something, you need more surface learning; as you get more surface knowledge, you move to deep learning.

In this chapter, we will examine the importance of surface literacy learning and consider the use of high-impact approaches that foster initial acquisition and consolidation. As we noted in the first chapter, almost everything in published research works at least some of the time with some students. Our challenge as a profession is to become more precise in what we do and when we do it. Timing is everything, and the wrong practice at the wrong time undermines efforts. Knowing when to help a student move from surface to deep is one of the marks of expert teachers. Literacy practices that foster deep learning, as discussed in the following chapter, are not necessarily the most effective ones to employ when students are still at the surface level of literacy learning.

Why Surface Literacy Learning Is Essential

In retrospect, this was obvious, yet we didn't understand it at the time. Nancy recalls working with seasoned teachers to develop new knowledge and skills about problem-based learning (PBL). She held workshops, engaged in professional reading and discussions, and hosted a professional learning community focused on the practice. Yet time and again, the effort fizzled as teachers said it didn't work. They blamed their students' existing knowledge, lack of motivation, and inability to engage in self-directed learning. PBL, they said, didn't work, full stop. Yet problem-based learning can work, under the right conditions. However—and this is critical—it isn't particularly effective when students don't yet possess the knowledge, skills, and dispositions needed to engage an inquiry-driven investigation about a topic. In other words, the timing is off. PBL is better for deepening knowledge, but not for the initial surface learning needed in advance of such study. (This is mainly because it is introduced too early, before students have sufficient surface knowledge.)

EFFECT SIZE FOR PROBLEM-BASED LEARNING = 0.15

Hattie (2009) calls these the worlds of "ideas, thinking, and constructing" (p. 26). He further reinterprets these three worlds as surface, deep, and transfer learning. There has been much deserved criticism of surface (some would say superficial) learning at the expense of learning that deepens over time and leads to transfer to new and novel situations. It is about getting the balance between these three right, not one or the others. An examination of teacher questioning about reading comprehension reveals what is valued. Durkin's seminal analysis of the questioning habits of reading teachers, first published nearly four decades ago (1978–1979), has remained distressingly stable. She found that little in the way of comprehension instruction occurred, and instead the practice of "comprehension testing" by way of asking recall questions was the norm. As an example, Bintz and Williams (2005) examined the questioning habits of fifth- and sixth-grade reading teachers, and reported that 54% were at the basic recall level. These and other researchers have made the case that much of the testing conducted by states and provinces values recall and recognition of factual information, further reinforcing teachers' attention on the surface level of meaning.

While we are not defending the wholesale use of recall questions at the expense of those that foster critical and creative thinking, it is important to note *when and where* in the lesson sequence this is occurring. Van den Broek, Tzeng, Risden, Trabasso, and Basche (2001) studied the effects of inferential reading comprehension questioning on students in the fourth, seventh, and tenth grades, as well as on college undergraduates. They found that questions posed during the reading of the text aided in shifting attention to specific information for older and more proficient readers. However, it interfered with the comprehension of the fourth- and seventh-grade students, who performed better when the questions came after, not during, the reading. These younger students had to devote more cognitive resources to grasping the literal meaning of the text than the older, more proficient readers did. In other words, to simply state that inferential questions are good and recall questions are bad is wrong. Timing and context are vital considerations.

> To simply state that inferential questions are good and recall questions are bad is wrong. Timing and context are vital considerations.

By extension, placing the right amount of emphasis at the right time in the instructional sequence is essential. Balance is warranted. Above all, literacy teachers need to be clear about their goals across learning units, recognize how these goals transform across time, and clearly communicate these goals to students. That means that within and across units, learning moves from surface-level to deeper understanding, and hopefully students develop the ability to transfer knowledge and skills into new situations. As such, instruction needs to be attuned to where students are, and where they are headed, across these three major phases. Teachers pay a huge disservice to students when they stop the learning once the surface level is mastered.

In turn, we are equally at fault when we skim over this first phase and prematurely ask students to construct without the tools they need to do so. It also does not mean we have to bore the students, make them rote learn, and just focus on facts or definitions. Note, for example, the meta-analysis by Murphy, Wilkinson, Soter, Hennessey, and Alexander (2009), who found that some classrooms were highly effective at promoting students' literal and inferential comprehension. That is, many students began to develop the subject matter vocabulary by hearing other students in planned discussion.

Acquisition and Consolidation

Surface (and deep) learning consists of two subphases: acquisition and consolidation. Hattie (2012) argues that the pedagogical goal at the *acquisition* period is to help students summarize and outline the topic of study. The *consolidation* period leads to a second facet of learning, which is accomplished through practice testing and receiving feedback. We imagine this resonates with you at a fundamental level, in that it mirrors what we know about the science of learning. Students need to first acquire and then begin to consolidate the information. (The learning doesn't stop there, of course, but it's important to know where to begin.)

We'll use a nonacademic example of a universally relatable experience: learning to drive. It's likely that your introduction to driving took place at a safe distance from the vehicle. Whether in a driver education class (old school) or online (for our younger readers), the initial information you acquired concerned traffic laws and signage. Soon you were behind the wheel in a protected environment, and someone introduced you to steering, taught you how to set and check mirrors, and showed you how to operate the gearshift and brakes. All of this knowledge and skill was surface acquisition, in that you gained a general sense of the territory, and were able to summarize basic information and outline the steps of the driving process. At this time, telling you about defensive driving, how to anticipate other driver actions, or the mechanics of the clutch would be of limited use; you just want to know the basics.

But being able to correctly identify the brake and accelerator pedals is not driving. You were now faced with having to consolidate the information. Figuring out how to operate the car while taking into account the traffic laws, signage, and changing conditions takes lots of time.

You had lots of practice testing—low stakes—to refine your ability to apply the right amount of pressure to the pedals in order to regulate your speed. And you got immediate feedback from the vehicle (remember that noise when you ground the gears?). Some of us may recall the terrified expression on the face of the well-meaning adult who sat in the passenger seat. We all know the reaction of parent instructors who rushed this early surface stage and could not understand why their child made such "obvious" mistakes—you need to overlearn many basic surface tasks before starting to get fancy! Consolidating freshly acquired knowledge and skills takes time, repetition, practice, rehearsal, and feedback. Looking back on our early driving careers, we know now we weren't ready to hit the highway under challenging road conditions. We were only at the level of surface consolidation, not deep consolidation. We will explore instructional approaches to deep acquisition and deep consolidation of literacy learning in the next chapter.

> Evaluating one's impact on learners is a key principle of visible learning.

Now let's put ourselves in the shoes of that well-meaning adult. If we had successful early driving experiences, it's attributable in large part to the skill of the person who was teaching us. He or she broke down complex skills into manageable parts, scaffolded understanding, and provided feedback. Most of all, that person evaluated his or her impact by measuring your success. If you didn't perform a three-point turn correctly, that person knew the instruction needed to change. If he was skilled at this, he didn't say, "I've taught seven other people how to drive, and I am going to stick with this strategy even though I have evidence it isn't working with you." In other words, he didn't remain obstinately attached to a strategy at the expense of your learning. Instead, he adjusted his approach based on your achievement of desired results. Your learning was visible because of the way you were operating the car and because the driving teacher was paying attention and evaluating his impact on your learning. The practice of continually evaluating one's impact on learners is a key principle of visible learning (Hattie, 2009, 2012).

Acquisition of Literacy Learning Made Visible

Teaching students to read, write, speak, and listen is hard and complex work. And we're not just referring to the basic skills needed to decode and encode. We want our students to leverage these skills in ways that allow them to gain knowledge, critically analyze ideas, express themselves, and create new knowledge that can be used by others. It would be wrong-headed to think that acquisition is something to be relegated to discrete decoding and encoding skills. Kindergarten students can engage in both discrete skill development and complex thinking, provided they have had sufficient time and expert instruction on how to gain knowledge, critically analyze ideas, and so on. Each of these *begins* with the acquisition phase of instruction. In this section of the chapter, we will discuss literacy acquisition practices that yield effect sizes worthy of our time:

- Leveraging prior knowledge

- Phonics and direct instruction

- Vocabulary instruction

- Reading comprehension in context

Remember that at this early stage of literacy learning, our pedagogical goal is for students to be able to stake out the territory by summarizing and outlining the key landmarks of the unit of study. Two important reminders are key to visible literacy learning:

1. **The teacher clearly signals the learning intentions and success criteria** to ensure that students know what they are learning, why they are learning it, and how they will know they have learned it, and to maximize the opportunity for students to be involved in the learning.

2. **The teacher does not hold any instructional strategy in higher esteem than his or her students' learning**. Visible teaching is a continual evaluation of one's impact on students' learning. When the evidence suggests that learning has not occurred, the instruction needs to change (not the student!).

Leveraging Prior Knowledge

What a student already knows about a topic is an excellent predictor of how that child will perform in subsequent assessments of writing (Chesky

& Hiebert, 1987), reading comprehension (McNamara & Kintsch, 1996), and word identification (Priebe, Keenan, & Miller, 2012). By extension, the effect size of a student's prior achievement—that is, his or her performance in learning—is significant. Although a teacher may have no influence over the knowledge a student has acquired in the past, the teacher has significant influence on how it will be leveraged. However, doing so requires

1. Knowing what the student already knows

2. Teaching with the intention to build on and extend the student's knowledge

We have noted before that the knowledge students bring to reading, and what we do (or do not do) with it, is "the missing piece of the comprehension puzzle" (Fisher & Frey, 2009, p. 1).

Possessing prior knowledge is one thing; knowing what to do with it is another. What students already know about a topic may be jumbled, disorganized, and incomplete—and sometimes it can be plain wrong. Teachers can assess the prior knowledge of their students using tools such as anticipation guides (Tierney, Readance, & Dishner, 1995). Anticipation guides, such as the example in Figure 2.1, are designed to determine what students know, and are especially effective when they hone in on common misconceptions. Janice Hightower, an 11th-grade U.S. history teacher, used this anticipation guide to determine what her students knew, or believed they knew, about the U.S. Constitution in advance of their study of the document.

"Every year I have a number of students who believe they know a lot about it because they have come into contact with it so many times. But there are some big misconceptions about what this document actually says," she explained.

Rather than focus on isolated facts, she chose five statements that focused on broader understanding of the piece. "Only numbers 1 and 4 are true statements," she said. "I'm interested in their reasoning, and I ask them to complete this before, and then again after, we have discussed this. I want them to see how their thinking has shifted in light of their learning."

EFFECT SIZE
FOR PRIOR
ACHIEVEMENT
= 0.65

ANTICIPATION GUIDE FOR U.S. CONSTITUTION DOCUMENT ANALYSIS

Directions: Read each statement and answer true or false.

Before Reading	Statement	After Reading
	1. The document was ratified more than a decade after the colonies went to war with Great Britain.	
	2. It states that there must be a "separation of church and state."	
	3. It guarantees everyone the right to vote.	
	4. It can be changed by passage of an amendment.	
	5. Public education is a guaranteed right.	

Explain why each statement is true or false.

Before Reading	After Reading
1.	1.
2.	2.
3.	3.
4.	4.
5.	5.

Figure 2.1

 Template available for download at **http://resources.corwin.com/VL-Literacy**

At this early stage of literacy learning, our pedagogical goal is for students to be able to stake out the territory by summarizing and outlining the key landmarks of the unit of study.

Another method for ascertaining prior knowledge is a cloze procedure (Taylor, 1953). Originally designed as a means for measuring text readability, this method has been utilized to determine a student's prior knowledge as well as syntactical control. The classic procedure calls for the use of a 250-word text passage, with every fifth word removed. The first and last sentences are left intact to provide context to the reading. Students read and fill in each blank with the word they believe is missing. The teacher compares each student's results against the original text, substitutions and synonyms notwithstanding. Teachers of younger children and English learners may select shorter passages, and choose to delete every seventh or ninth word in order to have longer strings of meaningful text in place. Because of the strict adherence to the exact word match, cut scores are low:

- Independent level: 60% or more correct answers

- Instructional level: 40%–59% correct

- Frustration level: 39% or below correct

Fourth-grade teacher Angelina Lamar-Henderson creates a cloze using a summary passage from her science textbook in advance of her unit of study. "The end of the unit always has an excellent summary of the key ideas, so I use that. I delete every seventh word, and the passage is usually about 150 words long."

Before teaching a unit on conservation and transfer of energy, she administered the cloze to determine what her students knew and did not know. "I don't give them a word bank, because many of them can figure out what to plug in due to the syntax clues," she said. None of her students scored at the independent level, meaning that none of them could already demonstrate mastery. While the majority of her students scored at the instructional level, six were at the frustration level.

"There's my red flag," she said. "That tells me that I need to build the background knowledge they'll need to be successful for this unit."

Throughout the unit, Ms. Lamar-Henderson met more frequently in teacher-directed small group instruction to preteach concepts, and checked in with them more frequently to gauge their progress. "I'll always have children who have knowledge gaps, but it's surprising how much of a shift there is from one unit to the next. I've learned not to assume, 'once a successful learner, always a successful learner.'"

By keeping close tabs on the impact of her instruction, Ms. Lamar-Henderson is accelerating her students' learning.

Phonics Instruction and Direct Instruction in Context

The acquisition, consolidation, and deepening of reading skills requires intentional instruction that extends across K–12 schooling. Although typically developing human infants and toddlers will acquire spoken language through complex interactions with the environment, not all will learn to read. The human brain is hardwired to learn to speak, due to evolutionary processes that evolved anywhere from 1.75 million to 50,000 years ago (Uomini & Meyer, 2013). But the act of reading is an invention, one that is only about 6,000 years old, and every brain must be trained to utilize spoken language structures to do the work of reading (Dehaene, 2009). This appropriation of neuronal structures requires specific intervention—we call it reading instruction. The complex act of reading involves six major facets that over time consolidate

- **Phonemic awareness:** The sounds of the language
- **Alphabetics:** The symbols of the language
- **Phonics:** The ability to bolt the sounds of the language onto its symbols
- **Fluency:** The ability to decode running text with automaticity
- **Vocabulary:** The denotative and connotative meanings of words and phrases
- **Reading comprehension:** Application and integration of strategies to sustain and regain meaning over longer pieces of text

Reading researcher Scott Paris (2005) describes these as a collection of constrained and unconstrained skills. Constrained reading skills are those that have boundaries or limits. There are 44 phonemes in English, and 26 letters. As well, there are a finite number of letter combinations that represent the sounds. And there is a limit as to the rate of reading one can sustain without sacrificing accuracy and meaning. These first four reading skills—phonemic awareness, alphabetics, phonics, and fluency—are constrained reading skills. Because we can count them, they are easily measured, and more importantly, they are the foundational reading skills all young readers need to acquire.

However, the ability to decode and read text fluently is not the final destination. If so, we wouldn't need to do much instruction beyond third grade for the first three constrained skills and eighth grade for the fourth. But true reading is much more than accurate word calling. All of us spend a lifetime acquiring what Paris calls the unconstrained reading skills of vocabulary and comprehension. Unlike constrained skills, there is no endpoint. Your vocabulary is better today than it was five years ago, and your reading comprehension will be better five years from now.

> All of us spend a lifetime acquiring what Paris calls the unconstrained reading skills of vocabulary and comprehension. Unlike constrained skills, there is no endpoint.

Effective reading instruction involves both constrained and unconstrained skills development. No responsible primary teacher would limit attention to constrained skills only, while ignoring vocabulary and reading comprehension. But constrained skills do have a shelf life, in that once they are learned, they no longer need to be taught. Therefore, attention to constrained skills instruction does fade after the first years of school as students acquire them. In turn, vocabulary and reading comprehension take on an even more prominent role than in the primary years.

EFFECT SIZE FOR PHONICS INSTRUCTION = 0.54

The role and importance of phonics instruction and direct instruction should be considered within the context of constrained and unconstrained skills. As such, the mastery of the constrained skills of the sounds and letters of the language are foundational, as is the ability to increasingly consolidate this knowledge to accurately and smoothly decode running text. Although phonics instruction and direct instruction do not encapsulate everything novice readers need to know, they build a gateway to a lifetime of reading. Phonics instruction, which is composed of the sounds, letters, and letter combinations that represent those sounds, is critical for beginning readers. Unlike spoken language, young children will not simply absorb these skills through exposure.

Phonics instruction is thought to establish and strengthen the brain structures that will form the phonological loop that links the apparatus responsible for processing the sounds of language with the long-term memory needed to sustain meaningful reading (Swanson, 1999a).

The surface acquisition phase of constrained reading skills is critical. When instruction around these skills is haphazardly administered, student learning is undermined. There are some things that have to be directly explained to students, especially when other methods are less effective or more time consuming. But the phrase *direct instruction* may cause initial concern among educators who fear that it means that a didactic, rigid, and lecturing approach is what is necessary. Formal direct instruction should not be used as the sole means for teaching reading (Ryder, Burton, & Silberg, 2006) any more than vocabulary should be the sole focus of the curriculum. Having said that, direct instruction can be an effective method for teaching the constrained skills (e.g., Swanson, 1999b). The effect size of direct instruction curriculum is high at 0.59.

EFFECT SIZE FOR DIRECT INSTRUCTION = **0.59**

Importantly, the features of direct instruction apply more broadly and include key elements of the lesson design:

- The teacher should plan according to the **learning intentions. Student engagement and commitment** is built through discussion of the learning intentions, success criteria, and tasks.

- The teacher **presents the lesson** using modeling and frequent checks for understanding.

- **Guided instruction** occurs such that the teacher is able to provide scaffolds and feedback to move the student toward independence.

- The teacher knows the **success criteria** and utilizes the results to analyze the impact of the teaching on student learning.

- **Closure** of the direct instruction portion of the lesson occurs such that students revisit the learning intentions and success criteria, as well as the key learning points.

- **Independent learnin**g continues as students apply newly learned knowledge to new, but parallel, situations.

Fifth-grade teacher Marla O'Campo uses direct instruction when her learning intentions focus on acquisition of new knowledge or skills. She also knows that students need to practice and use that knowledge or those skills if they are going to generalize and transfer them to new situations. For example, when she analyzed a writing task, she noted that her students failed to include reasons for their ideas or opinions. She was pleased to see that her students were able to maintain a controlling idea throughout the writing and that the transitions were strong. But the lack of concrete reasons for their ideas was troubling. She assumed, incorrectly, that students had been previously taught to include reasons for their opinions. She used a direct instruction approach to focus her students on including reasons. Her learning intention was "We can include reasons for any opinions we make in our writing." The success criteria she established with her students included using reasons that were real (as opposed to invented) or that came from the texts they were reading.

Ms. O'Campo then wrote a paragraph in the presence of her students, modeling her thinking as she did so. She wrote a short text that included her opinion about why some people fail to recycle. As she wrote, she included an example from her recent visit to a local park as well as a quote from the text the class had been reading. As part of their practice, Ms. O'Campo asked her students to help her with the second paragraph. She wrote the first line and then asked students to individually write a line on their paper that would work for her. She provided them with sentence frames:

1. Specifically, _____.
   (provide an example or detail here)

2. For example, _____.
   (provide an example or detail here)

3. As a matter of fact, _____.
   (provide an example or detail here)

> Constrained skills do have a shelf life, in that once they are learned, they no longer need to be taught.

Video 2.1
Direct Instruction:
Punctuating Dialogue

*http://resources.corwin.com/
VL-Literacy*

Following this, she asked students to revisit the learning intention and work on their own papers, incorporating reasons for the ideas and opinions they had. She reminded them of the success criteria and set them on their way.

Vocabulary Instruction

In the previous section, we discussed the importance of constrained skills instruction to build the foundational skills needed for meaningful reading. But constrained skills instruction alone fails to provide students with the tools they need for mature reading, and especially for transfer. Chief among unconstrained skills is vocabulary. Vocabulary knowledge is a strong predictor of reading comprehension (Baker, Simmons, & Kame'enui, 1998; Stahl & Fairbanks, 1986), and at the 0.67 effect size, strong vocabulary programs fall well into the zone of desired effects. Reading researcher Biemiller (2005), in his report on the choice and sequence of vocabulary words taught to young readers, reminds us that "[t]eaching vocabulary will not guarantee success in reading, just as learning to read words will not guarantee success in reading. However, lacking either adequate word identification skills or adequate vocabulary will ensure failure" (p. 223). However, vocabulary instruction, like other aspects of the curriculum, must be taught for depth and transfer. Unfortunately, too many children and adolescents experience vocabulary instruction as making passing acquaintances with a wide range of words. They know that many of the words won't be used again, and that next week there will be a new list.

> EFFECT SIZE
> FOR VOCABULARY
> PROGRAMS = **0.67**

So what does it mean to know a word? Vocabulary knowledge should be viewed across five dimensions (Cronbach, 1942, cited in Graves, 1986):

- **Generalization** through definitional knowledge
- **Application** through correct usage
- **Breadth** through recall of words
- **Precision** through understanding examples and nonexamples
- **Availability** through use of vocabulary in discussion

We chose to address vocabulary instruction within the context of surface acquisition, knowing that teachers should never stop at simply exposing students to vocabulary. Learning a word requires not just exposure, but also repetition, contextualization, and authentic reasons to use the terminology in discussion, reading, and writing. We will return to the topic of vocabulary through the next few chapters, and we discuss deepening knowledge and fostering transfer of this unconstrained skill, while acknowledging that the starting point of vocabulary instruction is in knowing which words and phrases deserve to be taught. Too often, vocabulary selection is a hit-or-miss process, with some teachers identifying all the multisyllabic and rare words in a reading, while others cling to a list of words from the past. We suggest a decision-making process that considers the features of the word and the likelihood that the term or phrase will be acquired through other means, such as repetition or analysis. Only those that cannot be learned through these means are taught through direct instruction. Figure 2.2 presents the questions we pose, based on the work of Graves (2006), Nagy (1988), and Marzano and Pickering (2005).

"It took me quite a few years to realize I was relying too much on direct telling of students when it came to vocabulary," said eighth-grade English teacher Diego Flores. "I took the problem solving away from them, and I made them depend on me too much."

Teachers like Mr. Flores recognize that students will not develop strategies for resolving unknown words and phrases if they have limited reasons to do so. "I used to do a lot more spoon-feeding. I'd take all the challenging words and define every one of them before my students ever read anything."

Mr. Flores has become more strategic about limiting his direct telling to words and phrases that are important to understanding a text or concept, but that don't offer other possibilities for resolution. "My school has devoted more time to teaching key roots and bases so that students can draw on a larger bank of derivations," he said. "For us at the middle school, we're focused on Latin and Greek roots so they understand the patterns in words."

A DECISION-MAKING MODEL FOR SELECTING VOCABULARY FOR DIRECT INSTRUCTION

Condition	Questions to Ask
Representative	• Is the word representative of a family of words the student will need to know?
	• Is the word or phrase representative of a concept the student will need to know?
If yes, proceed to next section.	
Transportable	• Will the word or phrase be needed in discussion, reading, and/or writing tasks?
If yes, proceed to next section. Now determine how the word will be acquired.	
Frequency	• Does the word or phrase appear frequently in the text?
Contextual Analysis	• Does the word or phrase present an opportunity for the student to apply contextual analysis skills to resolve word meaning?
Structural Analysis	• Does the word or phrase present an opportunity for the student to apply structural analysis skills to resolve word meaning?
If the word appears frequently, and presents opportunities to resolve word meaning using contextual or structural analysis, the word probably does not need direct instruction. If the word is essential, and yet cannot be resolved through frequent use, contextual analysis, or structural analysis, the word or phrase should be introduced through direct instruction.	

Figure 2.2

In addition to direct telling of vocabulary words, there are some other ways to develop students' understanding of academic terminology. We will provide examples using mnemonics, word cards, modeling word solving, word and concept sorts, and wide reading.

Mnemonics

How often have you used this strategy (even if you couldn't name it) to recall a string of words—"Roy G. Biv" to remember the colors of the light spectrum (red, orange, yellow, green, blue, indigo, and violet), or

EFFECT SIZE FOR
MNEMONICS = 0.45

"HOMES" to recall the names of the U.S. Great Lakes (Huron, Ontario, Michigan, Erie, and Superior)? A mnemonic device is a memory aid used to link a string of words together. Songs are used with small children to learn the names of the letters of the alphabet, or to recall phonics rules such as "when two vowels go walking, the first one does the talking." Although mnemonic devices do not deepen knowledge, they are quite helpful when students are initially acquiring information they need to recall. In addition to name and musical mnemonics, other techniques include using an image, or an expression ("Every Good Boy Does Fine" to recall that the notes of the musical scale are E, G, B, D, and F).

Word Cards

Yessenia Cordova uses word cards developed by her students using the Frayer method (Frayer, Frederick, & Klausmeier, 1969) to learn new vocabulary. Her sixth-grade students divide a 4 × 6 index card into four quadrants and write the targeted word in the upper left-hand quadrant. The definition, written in the students' own words after the teacher explains the meaning, is included in the upper right-hand corner. Next, they write a nonexample or opposite of the word in the bottom right-hand corner. In the bottom left-hand corner, the students illustrate the meaning of the word. The image mnemonic they choose is vital, and is thought to embed newly learned information into a visual memory students can retrieve. Ms. Cordova explained, "I ask students to create these word cards as I introduce new terms for them, and then they use these for rehearsal and memorization." An example of Jamal's word card for *sonnet* appears in Figure 2.3.

Modeling Word Solving

How often have you wished you could see in the mind of someone who is an expert at what he or she does? Perhaps it is an athlete, or a musician, or a chess player. We mention these specific examples because they have been the subject of studies about the differences between experts and novices (Bransford, Brown, & Cocking, 2000). The expert in the classroom is often, but not always, the teacher. Like the athlete, musician,

Sonnet

a poem with 14 lines. It's a "little song"

open verse poem that doesn't rhyme

Figure 2.3

or chess player, he or she is able to notice, coordinate, and respond to subtle changes in systems. Moreover, many possess the ability to tap into their cognitive and metacognitive processes. In other words, not only do they know what to do, but they also know why and how they are doing it. Unfortunately, all of this insight may stay locked away and out of sight from the ones who might otherwise benefit most.

The act of teacher modeling and thinking aloud allows students to see inside the mind of the teacher to discover how decisions are made. Importantly, this includes possible strategies that are considered and discarded. It is useful for them to see that we rapidly move through several prospects before settling on an approach. This is particularly useful when students are acquiring knowledge for the purpose of solving a problem. Nowhere is this more true than when a reader is confronted by an unknown word or phrase. A think-aloud about how one resolves this problem is much more useful than telling the learner to "look it up in the dictionary."

We teach our students how to resolve such discrepancies using a three-part heuristic, and regularly model how we apply it (Frey & Fisher, 2009):

- Look inside the word or phrase for structural clues.

- Look outside the word or phrase for contextual clues.

- Look further outside the word or phrase for resources.

Fourth-grade teacher Tim Williams did just that when he was reading aloud an informational text passage in a science unit on habitats:

> The vegetation is the plant life that we find growing in a region. We call these large regions of the earth biomes. Biomes can be compared to very large ecosystems. (S&S Learning, 2013, p. 25)

The teacher paused and said, "That word *biome* caught me off guard, and I stumbled over it. But then I saw that it is really part of a phrase—*earth biome*. The first thing I do when I run into a word that I'm not really sure of is to look inside the word to see if I can take it apart. I can see that *bio-* is in there, and I know *bio-* means life. Remember when we studied biographies and autobiographies? That's the story of a person's life. So I'll put that together. *Earth life*. Hmm, not a whole lot of help, so now I'll go back and look outside the word for context clues. Earlier in the sentence, it says a biome is a region. And the sentence before talks about the vegetation. The sentence that follows says biomes can be compared to ecosystems. But now I have another question. Is a biome only about the vegetation? I know an ecosystem includes the animals and insects, too. I'll have to keep reading to find out. I could also look in the glossary in the back, but for now I'm going to read a little further before I decide to do that. If this isn't cleared up for me soon, I'll look it up."

Word and Concept Sorts

It is human nature that we actively seek out patterns to help us make sense of the world, and vocabulary sorts make the most of this. Word sorts require children to categorize similar terms using a critical feature: a sound, spelling pattern, or, in the case of concept sorts, meaning. These are used most commonly at the elementary level, and help students to develop the orthographic, decoding, and vocabulary skills needed for reading and writing (Bear, Invernizzi, Templeton, & Johnston, 2011). First-grade teacher Kiely O'Neill leads her students through sorting activities as she introduces new spelling words. She is teaching the consonant–vowel–consonant–silent *e* (CVCe) spelling pattern, and introduces words such as *cape, fame, kite, mole,* and *rule*. She also includes several other words that do not use this pattern, such as *hat, cob,* and *tree*. After introducing the spelling rule, she and the children sort out the words into two columns.

> Word sorts help students to process their thinking aloud.

"Let's look again at the words that have that CVCe pattern to make sure we've got them all in the correct category," she says. They initially are not sure where to put *tree*, since it ends with an /e/, but soon settle on its correct placement.

"The word sorts help them to process their thinking aloud so they can figure out the problem," Ms. O'Neill told us.

Sixth-grade English teacher Hal Franklin uses a similar approach for very different purposes. His students are sorting terms according to concepts rather than spelling patterns. Working in pairs, students are sorting terms according to whether they are literary devices or poetic techniques. Terms such as *allegory, foreshadowing,* and *theme* are part of the first category, while *verse, alliteration,* and *repetition* belong in the second. The conversation really gets going when the partners have to decide what goes in a third column: techniques used in both. Most quickly settle on *simile* and *metaphor*, but speculate about others such as *imagery* and *personification*. "It gives me the opportunity to expand their original definitions of these terms, some of which they learned in elementary school. Now they have to think across genres. It heightens their awareness of the author's or poet's craft," he said.

Wide Reading

Among all the methods used to expand student vocabulary, few compare to wide reading. Young children who are regularly read to post higher levels of vocabulary knowledge (Snell, Hindman, & Wasik, 2015). Older children who read regularly are in turn exposed to words they might not ever hear in everyday speech (Beck, McKeown, & Kucan, 2013). The importance of choice and volume cannot be overstated here: students who have more choices in what they read will read more (Guthrie & Wigfield, 2000). Children who read for more minutes each day are exposed to a higher volume of words, which in turn correlates to higher levels of achievement (Anderson, Wilson, & Fielding, 1988).

Teachers like Davinia Johnson make sure that their classroom is filled with books and magazines for their students to choose from. Ms. Johnson sets aside time for her students to engage with the texts. "There are times when I have a specific list of books to choose from. They're usually related to what we're studying," she said. "But I also make sure that I've got books that they want to read, just because."

Thumbing through the books on her shelves reveals a host of terms that wouldn't be likely to come up anywhere but on the pages of a book. "They learn words like *saunter*. When would that ever come up unless it was on the page of a book?" she asked. Best of all, she noted, they are learning the words in context. "It's not a list of words. No one could directly teach them the number of words they need to know. They need lots of exposure to language to get to the 88,000 words they're supposed to know by the end of eighth grade," she said. "Reading is one of the best ways for them to do so."

Reading Comprehension Instruction in Context

Teaching reading comprehension is not a singular phenomenon, but rather is achieved through the use of a host of instructional practices designed to equip students with the ability to organize and analyze knowledge; link it to information about the social, biological, and physical worlds; reflect upon it; and take action. Like vocabulary, reading comprehension is fundamental in moving from surface to deep knowledge and transfer. The ultimate goal is for students to become integrative readers, not strategic ones. In other words, we hope students don't stop their reading to force a prediction or visualization but rather engage in these cognitive processes automatically. However, strategy instruction is an important first step in apprenticing students into approaches that can help them resolve issues when comprehension breaks down. Over time, readers increasingly integrate these into their reading and become more self-directed.

Summarizing

You will recall from earlier in this chapter that the goals during the surface acquisition phase of instruction are for students to be able to take stock of the broad outlines of the area of study. We know they don't have the fine-grained details down yet, but it is useful to have a larger conceptual map in mind, however spotty, when examining the nuances. Summarization is useful for students acquiring new knowledge because they "must build hierarchies of knowledge on a firm basis of accurate text representation" (Guthrie & Klauda, 2014, p. 395). In other words, it contributes to their overall reading compre- hension, and as such is an important strategy for this unconstrained skill. When students construct written summaries of texts, discussions, and concepts, they engage in an immediate review process that allows them to notice their own level of understanding, and receive timely and actionable feedback. Teachers like Tyrell Washington integrate summary opportunities regularly into his sixth-grade class. "Ancient world history gets pretty complex for them," Mr. Washington said. "I've noticed that they get buried in the dates, names, and places we discuss, and miss out on the big picture. But I didn't really know how often that happened until I started having them write short summaries a couple of times each period."

Like many teachers, he had previously done this exclusively at the end of class—"a ticket out the door," he explained. "I definitely got good feedback that I could take action on the next day, but I got more concerned about early in the unit, when all the information is new." Mr. Washington started asking students to write short summaries of a few sentences throughout his early unit lessons so he could respond more quickly.

Like vocabulary, reading comprehension is fundamental in moving from surface to deep knowledge and transfer.

"I'll give you an example from yesterday," he said. "We're studying Pompeii right now, and when I had them summarize what we had discussed and read about, quite a few of them still thought the place was overrun by lava. That was their internal model for how volcanoes work, and they missed the point that it was the intense heat and gases that killed so many people," said the social studies teacher. "I had to fix that right away, and I could because they were writing these short summaries halfway through the lesson."

Annotating Text

A challenge that many struggling readers face when summarizing text is that they are less accurate in determining the key ideas presented. Winograd (1984) studied the summaries of good and poor eighth-grade readers and noted that the students who struggled more often identified phrases and sentences containing "rich visual details that perhaps captured their interest. In contrast, more fluent readers seemed to be defining importance more in terms of textual importance" (p. 411). As texts become more complex, central ideas and key details are often scattered among several sentences, rather than definitely stated in a single sentence. Guided annotation of text, including underlining, circling, and making margin notes, can improve student understanding of new knowledge, and builds the capacity of students to better engage in study skills (study skills, including things like annotation, have an effect size of 0.63). It is important to state that teaching such skills in isolation of content (e.g., a study skills class) is not likely to deliver desired results.

EFFECT SIZE
FOR STUDY
SKILLS = 0.63

"We look for sentences that have the main idea all the time," said third-grade teacher Sara Wilkes. "When I'm doing a shared reading with them, I put the reading on the document camera, and we read it the first time to get the flow. Then we go back through and start talking about the main idea."

Her students have their own copies of the reading to annotate, and Ms. Wilkes moves back and forth between modeling and thinking aloud about main ideas, questions about the text, and connections to other ideas and texts, and then guiding students to locate these on their own and in small groups.

"It depends on where I am in the learning process," she said. "If we're still acquiring new information, I'm going to model how I locate the main idea and the key details. As we go deeper, I start shifting this responsibility to them. My goal is that they're increasingly able to do this on their own, even when I don't ask."

Note-Taking

Another facet within the broader context of study skills that improve comprehension is note-taking. Note-taking is the practice of translating and transcribing key points during a lecture, while note-making (sometimes called text extraction) is done during reading. While the act of taking notes during class makes sense, especially when acquiring new information, its true value is more apparent when you consider how studying one's notes aids in deepening knowledge, and organizing and transforming information for transfer.

EFFECT SIZE FOR TAKING CLASS NOTES = **0.59**

EFFECT SIZE FOR ORGANIZING AND TRANSFORMING = **0.85**

A common method for teaching secondary students about note-taking is the Cornell method (Pauk & Owens, 2010), originally designed by Walter Pauk when he was the director of the reading and study center at Cornell University. Using this method, students learn to divide their notes into three sections (see Figure 2.4 on the next page), then use them to practice the "6 *Rs*":

1. **Record** the lecture notes in the main section of the note page.

2. **Reduce** the essential ideas by reviewing the notes within 24 hours and phrasing these ideas as questions.

3. **Recite** the information aloud by answering these questions while keeping the notes portion covered.

4. **Reflect** by asking oneself about how well the material is understood, and what clarifying questions should be asked of the teacher.

5. **Review** during subsequent short study sessions.

6. **Recapitulate** the main ideas by writing them in the summary section.

FORMAT FOR CORNELL NOTES

Cues	Notes
For main ideas	Record lecture notes here during class
Phrased as questions	Use meaningful abbreviations and symbols
Written within 24 hours after class	Leave space to add additional information

Summary
Main ideas and major points are recorded here
These are written during later review sessions

Source: Pauk & Owens (2010).

Figure 2.4

Middle school English teacher Donna Scott introduces her students to Cornell note-taking at the beginning of the year. Her students initially have difficulty in figuring out what to put down, because she doesn't allow them to copy the presentation slides. Instead, she switches off the display and encourages them to discuss the main points with her and their classmates. "This is always a little rough at first, because they're used to copying, but not thinking. It's a real strain on their listening skills."

However, she really sees them beginning to get the hang of it when she hosts collaborative study sessions. "That's when they really begin to see exactly what information they would have liked to have written down, and what they didn't actually need," said Ms. Scott.

Importantly, she doesn't hold study sessions too early in the learning progression, when students are still acquiring knowledge. "We use them to study a few days after the fact, when they are moving into the consolidation phase of learning. I learn a lot from them, too. I get to hear what is sticking and what isn't, and adjust accordingly."

Consolidation of Literacy Learning Made Visible

Surface learning of literary skills and concepts is more than just introduction; students also need the time and space to begin to consolidate their new learning. It is through this early consolidation that they can begin to retrieve information and apply it in more sophisticated ways that will deepen their learning. However, the process of consolidation and recall of new information is surprising. Although it would be logical to assume that recall of new information right after it is taught would be higher than 24 hours later, it appears that the opposite is often the case (Henderson, Weighall, & Gaskell, 2013). The researchers found that initial word learning of elementary students was better a day later than it was immediately after they were taught, and that their recall was further strengthened when word meaning was taught. Time is also a factor in consolidation, and the opportunity to return to new learning again and again is further enhanced through rehearsal and memorization through spaced practice, receiving feedback, and collaborative learning with peers (Hattie, 2012).

> The opportunity to return to new learning again and again is further enhanced through rehearsal and memorization through spaced practice, receiving feedback, and collaborative learning with peers.

Rehearsal and Memorization Through Spaced Practice

Literacy learning—whether it be speaking, listening, reading, or writing—benefits from the same kinds of techniques used to master other complex skills. This means that students need to regularly have the occasion to rehearse what they have learned. We cannot overestimate the importance of this consolidation—in many senses, the purpose is to "overlearn" the

Video 2.2
Surface, Deep, and
Transfer Learning

*http://resources.corwin.com/
VL-Literacy*

surface knowing so that students can more readily access this information when they move to the deeper, comprehension, and inferential tasks.

Consider the many flash card games teachers of primary students use as drills to promote memorization. Kindergarten teacher Kevin Pritchard uses flash card games to promote sight word memorization. Importantly, he knows that these techniques are not especially effective during the initial acquisition phase of learning, but rather, "I wait until my students have had several exposures to these words. We talk about them; I point them out during shared readings; I write them in the daily news we discuss every day," he said.

The 220 Dolch sight words are service words that (1) appear frequently and (2) are more difficult to sound out. There are some nouns and verbs, but most are linking words such as *in*, *here*, *have*, and *them*. Memorization of these words contributes to a beginning reader's emergent fluency in reading and writing simple sentences. As automaticity grows, less cognitive space has to be devoted to decoding, and attention can shift to comprehension (LaBerge & Samuels, 1974).

Each day, Mr. Pritchard plays games such as My Pile, Your Pile, using these sight words; in this game, each correctly named word is placed in the child's pile, while those that are incorrect remain with the teacher. "The ones they get wrong become the ones that I use more frequently so that the children get more chances to rehearse," he explained. He uses an incremental rehearsal technique, interspersing the incorrect ones with flash cards they have mastered. "I keep it at about 20% unknown words and 80% known words so that I can keep their motivation level up," said the teacher. "I also keep these drills pretty short. Ten minutes tops for these little guys." Mr. Pritchard understands that practice that is distributed over longer periods of time is more effective than the mass practice of fewer but longer practice sessions.

Fourth-grade teacher Lindsay Yee uses a different form of rehearsal during her writer's workshop lessons. Her students engage in planning their writing using a variety of tools, including graphic organizers. Unlike many writing teachers, she uses recorded oral rehearsal of their writing before they begin to compose (Bogard & McMackin, 2012). Using their graphic organizers and planning notes, students record an oral version of the piece they intend to write, then listen to the recording to make changes.

"It's valuable to them to hear themselves in the act of rehearsing their writing," said Ms. Yee. "It gets them started with editing before they have even begun committing their ideas on paper or screen. What I've noticed is how often they end up changing their initial organizer because of some new insight into their composing process."

Repeated Reading

Fluency in reading moves from surface to deep as readers move from decoding to attention to meaning (Topping, 2006). In typically developing children, this consolidation process occurs in the early grades, but some children continue to struggle. An effective intervention for children and adolescents who have not yet gained sufficient fluency is the repeated reading technique (Samuels, 1979). In repeated reading, a student listens to a passage read aloud by the teacher, then reads it to himself or herself any number of times, then reads it aloud. Rate, accuracy, and prosody (intonation, pacing, and expressiveness) are calculated, and reported to the student, along with the elapsed time. The student then reads it again, with the goal of improving each of these elements. Middle school reading specialist Janae Morrison uses the repeated reading technique with struggling readers, and has advice for implementation.

> EFFECT SIZE FOR REPEATED READING PROGRAMS = 0.67

"The first tip I have is to choose a passage that's going to be engaging to the students. I don't use more than 200 words so that they get lots of opportunities to reread," she said. "I also remind them that the goal isn't to read as fast as they can. I tell them they don't want to sound like the guy at the end of the car commercials rattling off all the details," she laughed. "I make sure they see where their errors are, and the time they posted, as well as the goal for them."

The reading specialist uses the oral reading fluency norms published by Hasbrouck and Tindal (2006) to set goals with them (see Figure 2.5). "They like to chart their progress as they get better," she said. "I think that's motivating for them, too. Like, 'Can I top my last score?'"

ORAL READING FLUENCY NORMS FROM GRADES 1–8

Grade	Percentile	Fall WCPM	Winter WCPM	Spring WCPM
1	90		81	111
	75		47	82
	50		23	53
	25		12	28
	10		6	15
	SD		32	39
	Count		16,950	19,434
2	90	106	125	142
	75	79	100	117
	50	51	72	89
	25	25	42	61
	10	11	18	31
	SD	37	41	42
	Count	15,896	18,229	20,128
3	90	128	146	162
	75	99	120	137
	50	71	92	107
	25	44	62	78
	10	21	36	48
	SD	40	43	44
	Count	16,988	17,383	18,372
4	90	145	166	180
	75	119	139	152
	50	94	112	123
	25	68	87	98
	10	45	61	72
	SD	40	41	43
	Count	16,523	14,572	16,269

Figure 2.5

Grade	Percentile	Fall WCPM	Winter WCPM	Spring WCPM
5	90	166	182	194
	75	139	156	168
	50	110	127	139
	25	85	99	109
	10	61	74	83
	SD	45	44	45
	Count	16,212	13,331	15,292
6	90	177	195	204
	75	153	167	177
	50	127	140	150
	25	98	111	122
	10	68	82	93
	SD	42	45	44
	Count	10,520	9,218	11,290
7	90	180	192	202
	75	156	165	177
	50	128	136	150
	25	102	109	123
	10	79	88	98
	SD	40	43	41
	Count	6,482	4,058	5,998
8	90	185	199	199
	75	161	173	177
	50	133	146	151
	25	106	115	124
	10	77	84	97
	SD	43	45	41
	Count	5,546	3,496	5,335

WCPM: Words correct per minute

SD: Standard deviation

Count: Number of student scores

Source: Hasbrouck & Tindal (2006). Used with permission.

Receiving Feedback

A repeating theme you will read throughout this book is on the power of feedback to shape students' thinking. Feedback from the teacher and peers can provide learners with the information they need to move incrementally toward success. Of course, not all feedback is useful and constructive. Wiggins (1998) writes about feedback conditions across four dimensions: it must be

EFFECT SIZE FOR
FEEDBACK = **0.75**

1. **Timely.** The timing of the feedback is critical. During the surface acquisition phase, discussed earlier in this chapter, learners are getting initial exposure to new knowledge. Feedback may be premature, and reteaching may be more effective. But soon after surface-level acquisition learning, during the surface consolidation period, feedback is essential, because students are just now beginning to rehearse and practice.

2. **Specific.** We've all been buried in an avalanche of feedback that exceeded our present level of knowledge. Nancy recalls getting an overwhelming amount of feedback from her driving teacher, and needless to say, it all ended in tears. Looking back, the feedback the driving teacher gave her was specific about what to do next, but it was too much at one time, and well beyond Nancy's ability to listen to, process, and execute. Although not what the instructor intended, she froze and shut down, rather than persisted.

3. **Understandable to the Learner.** Useful feedback needs to be aligned to the level of the learner's knowledge. Hattie (2012) calls this "just in time, just for me" feedback, further noting that "feedback is most powerful . . . when it is related to the student's degree of proficiency (from novice to apprentice)" (p. 102).

4. **Actionable.** Feedback that is withheld until the summative assignment has been submitted, and with no possibility of revising and resubmitting, is neither timely nor actionable. Feedback that is vague ("Good job!") is not specific—and further, not understandable or actionable—as the student speculates on what exactly made it "good."

Consider the feedback opportunity Mr. Pritchard is creating when he is playing flash card games with his kindergartners. When they get a sight word wrong, he says, "This word is _____." Then he spells the word and names the word again, and says, "Say that word again." The feedback is immediate and actionable.

The high school English department where Iona Newman works uses short online quizzes to provide timely feedback. For instance, students read a chapter in the novel they have selected from a list of texts that provide understandings to an agreed-upon essential question, then check their understanding by logging on to the learning management system and answering three to five questions about the events, characters, and key details. When students answer incorrectly, they receive a corrective message that refers them back to the passage containing the information—not the answer, mind you, but feedback that shifts their attention back to the salient passage.

> Feedback that is withheld until the summative assignment has been submitted, and with no possibility of revising and resubmitting, is neither timely nor actionable.

Ms. Newman said, "We got the inspiration to do this through the TED-Ed videos we had been using [http://ed.ted.com]. There are lessons developed by other teachers that feature these 'checking for understanding' questions. The best part is that when they get it incorrect, the program automatically takes them back to the video so they can locate the answer. Our department thought, 'We could do the same thing with our readings.'" These are low-stakes events, and are not graded. Rather, students are recognized for their completion and corrections of the tasks. "We want them to get into the habit of looking back into texts to seek understanding," she said. "We don't want them to cling to this simplistic idea that you only need to read something once, and then rely only on your recall. We want them to reference the text as often as they need to."

Collaborative Learning With Peers

Students consolidate their understanding in the presence of peers through productive group work (Frey & Fisher, 2013b). Purposeful discussion of complex texts during the surface consolidation phase is an excellent way to provide access to readings. For example, students engaged in book club or literature circle discussions have the opportunity to clarify their

> EFFECT SIZE FOR COOPERATIVE VERSUS INDIVIDUALISTIC LEARNING = **0.59**

Video 2.3
Having Successful
Collaborative
Conversations

*http://resources.corwin.com/
VL-Literacy*

Students
consolidate their
understanding
in the presence
of peers through
productive
group work.

collective thinking. However, these discussions need to be structured such that there is a shared investment in the outcomes, including individual as well as group accountability for the task.

Ninth-grade English teacher Alisa Guanotta introduced a collaborative learning discussion protocol for her students at the beginning of the year. Many of her students are learning English as a subsequent language, and she discovered that the majority of her class hadn't had much previous experience with small group discussion.

She explained, "These aren't those 'turn to your partner' sharing activities. I want them to engage over a longer period of time with one another as they hash out what's happening in the book."

Given their lack of experience, she chose short stories for their literature circle discussions. She began by profiling a range of selections tied to the unit's essential question, "to get them making connections to themselves, the world, and other texts," Ms. Guanotta said.

For the essential question, "Who do you want to be? What do you want to be?" she did brief book talks about short stories, including, Jack London's "To Build a Fire," Amy Tan's "Fish Cheeks," and "Mirror Image" by Lena Coakley, about a girl who has had the world's first brain transplant. Students chose the short story they wanted to read, and met with their groups to discuss, using the protocol she designed to prepare for their meeting (see Figure 2.6). At the end of the literature circle, they handed in their own completed protocol, and talked about how the conversation had helped them understand the text more fully.

Rico said, "I got kinda confused on the part when the fire kept going out and the dog was just watching. But my group talked about the dog being smarter than the man. The dog knew it was too cold."

The English teacher kept the debriefing focused on the usefulness of the group in helping one another to understand. "I'll keep building their stamina to engage with longer pieces of text, and to work with their groups for longer periods of time," she said. "So much of what we do in this class is about understanding yourself as a learner, and as a contributor."

DISCUSSION NOTES FOR "WHO DO YOU WANT TO BE? WHAT DO YOU WANT TO DO?"

Name: _____ Date: _____

Title: _____ Period: _____

Group Members: _____

_____

Please have notes prepared in advance of your literature circle meetings. Use these questions to guide your note-making.

Discussion: What questions are you thinking about at the end of this reading? What are you wondering about? What is confusing or unclear?

Powerful passages: What sections of the text caught your attention? This could be something surprising, weird, or well said. Make a note of the page number and beginning words so you can read it to your group. Be sure to write why you chose it.

Connections: What personal events were you reminded of in this reading? Are there other books you have read that connect with this story? How?

Illustration: Make a simple picture or diagram that represents this reading to you. Remember that what's important is not your artistic ability—it's your ideas.

Figure 2.6

 Template available for download at **http://resources.corwin.com/VL-Literacy**

Conclusion

A strong start sets the stage for meaningful learning and powerful impacts. Teachers need to be mindful of the place their students are in the learning cycle. Surface learning sets the necessary foundation for the deepening knowledge and transfer that will come later. But there's the caveat: teaching for transfer must occur. Too often, learning ends at the surface level, as up to 90% of instructional time is devoted to conveying facts and procedures (Hattie, 2012). Bu the challenge is this: we can't overcorrect in the other direction, bypassing foundational knowledge in favor of critical and analytic thinking. Students need and deserve to be introduced to new knowledge and skills thoughtfully and with a great deal of expertise on the part of the teacher. And teachers need to recognize the signs that it is time to move forward from the surface acquisition and surface consolidation period.

When the learning is visible, students and teachers are in sync. Teachers signal their students about what is being taught, why it is important, and how they will both gauge success. Teachers use feedback to help their students consolidate their initial learning, watching and listening carefully for indicators that learners are ready to move forward, or need more time and practice. That adds up to a strong start for deepening students' literacy learning.

DEEP LITERACY LEARNING

3

Society prizes those who delve deeper into issues and problems that have vexed humankind. The ability to hang with a problem requires persistence and a certain amount of confidence in one's ability to eventually arrive at a solution. We could list any number of geniuses here, but keep in mind that at one point they were children. What happened to them, in and out of the classroom, that might have contributed to their willingness and ability to go deeper?

Chances are very good that somewhere along the way, their imaginations were sparked. We'd like to think it was a teacher who had a hand in doing so—perhaps a teacher who saw something in students they could not see in themselves. That teacher likely constructed learning experiences that were relevant and interesting to the learner. We're talking about not entertaining, but rather inspiring students to explore and begin to acquire information on their own. Of course, each of these geniuses had surface-level knowledge that he or she could use.

Two of us had a similar experience when we decided to enroll in a functional neuroimaging class at our university. We had attended an International Mind, Brain, and Education Society conference (www .imbes.org) and realized that we didn't understand some of the sessions because of our lack of surface knowledge about the images the presenters were sharing. We were excited to learn more about them and found a class that fit our schedules.

The first night of the class was magical. The professor asked each of the 13 students (11 full-time doctoral students in psychology plus us) why we were taking the class and what we hoped to gain from it. Following each person's introduction, the professor commented on the information shared and then made notes on the syllabus that was being projected on the screen in front of us. For example, when Nancy talked about her work with young children with autism, our professor added a note to the syllabus, deleting the note about cerebral palsy and changing it to autism. As he did so, he said, "There are all kinds of exceptionalities that we can study. I'll provide you with a lot of examples electronically. I left cerebral palsy on here from last semester because a student in the class had CP. Given Nancy's interest, I think we'll focus a bit more on autism this semester instead."

We left the first night of class highly motivated. We read the assigned readings, participated in online discussion boards, and talked with friends and family about our new academic pursuit. But it wasn't just the first night that was magical. We were invited into the learning each time. Our professor had a learning target each night that we discussed as a class for several minutes. We got to talk about why we were learning this content and how it fit into the overall topic. For example, early in the class, he said that we would be comparing various neuroimaging techniques to assess their relative strengths and weaknesses. He also let us know that "by the end of the class, you will be able to identify which technique for neuroimaging would be appropriate to answer your research questions." He then talked about his own research and the tools that he used, as well as why he used them. At the end of each class, he would present us with "takeaways," some of which he had prepared in advance and others that emerged as we were engaged in the work. Suffice it to say that each and every lesson we had with him was interesting and relevant, and we never felt intimidated, even though we arguably worked harder in that course than any other we had ever taken. Most of all, our learning about neuroimaging has continued in the years since the course ended, in large part because he equipped us with the tools we needed to continue to deepen our understanding of the topic. We were capable of going deeper because we had acquired the prerequisite surface knowledge. However, it was the professor's construction of the learning environment that ensured that we did so.

Moving From Surface to Deep

The concept of surface and deep learning dates back to researchers such as Marton and Säljö (1976) and Biggs (1999). Each has described these constructs as internal to the learner, but under the influence of the teacher and the context. Surface learners are described as relying on memorization and are concerned about failure; therefore, they are risk-averse. Deep learners, on the other hand, seek to interact with content and ideas, and actively link concepts and knowledge across content. But Lublin (2003) states:

> One of the major concepts to emerge from this research
> was the idea that students can take different approaches to

Video 3.1
Deeper Learning

*http://resources.corwin.com/
VL-Literacy*

learning. These approaches are not stable traits in individuals, although some students will tend towards taking a deep approach while others will tend towards taking a surface approach (Biggs, 1999). Rather, it is suggested that good teaching can influence students to take a deep approach, while poor teaching in the widest sense can pressure students to take a surface approach. Biggs defines good teaching as the encouragement of a deep approach to learning. (p. 3)

> If you turn too quickly to the next set o' facts, without giving students sufficient time and tools to go deeper, they will quickly learn that surface learning is what you value, and in turn, surface learning is all that you will get.

In other words, the classroom milieu can either encourage or discourage a learner from adopting a deep view of learning. A teacher who emphasizes (and assesses) surface learning will cultivate surface-level learners. On the other hand, teachers who encourage learners to plan, investigate, and elaborate on their learning will nurture deep learners. And the teacher who emphasizes a strategic mode will nurture students who learn when to be surface and when to be deep. Whatever you pay attention to is what your students will pay attention to. What you test is what your students will believe you value. As we described in the previous chapter, initial literacy learning is a necessary starting point as students begin to acquire and consolidate their surface-level knowledge. But if you turn too quickly to the next set o' facts, without giving students sufficient time and tools to go deeper, they will quickly learn that surface learning is what you value, and in turn, surface learning is all that you will get.

It is at this point that the handwringing begins, and the talk of "covering the curriculum" and adhering to a pacing guide comes to the forefront. But if we truly stand behind the belief that teaching is about impacting learning, rather than stuffing heads with facts, then we need to reexamine how the curriculum we are working with is constructed. In nearly every case, there is a spiral to the curriculum, and an expectation that students by the end of the year will be able to do more, in more knowledgeable ways, than they could at the beginning of the year. And when students are equipped to deepen their learning, the pace of learning quickens. Think of it this way: it needs to start slow in order to go fast.

Therefore, this chapter is about equipping students with the tools they need to become deep learners. We focus on practices that have strong effect sizes—actions that ensure that students demonstrate at least a year's worth of learning. The previous chapter focused on sound presentation of knowledge. This one shifts to methods for not simply facilitating, but *activating* students' literacy learning. Deep learners are able to think metacognitively, take action, discuss ideas, and see errors as a necessary part of learning. Hattie and Yates (2014) described this as System 2 learning, in contrast to System 1, or surface, learning:

> System 1 is fast and responds with immediacy; System 2 entails using time to "stop, look, listen, and focus" (Stanovich, 1999). More recently Daniel Kahneman (2011) wrote about the two systems he distinguished as "thinking slow" and "thinking fast." Slow thinking is System 2, which requires deep, challenging and sometimes "hurting" thinking. Fast thinking is System 1, which rapidly calls on knowledge to be used in thinking slow. The more we make learning automatic (like learning the times tables) the easier is it for us to devote our cognitive resources to System 2 deeper tasks (such as using the times tables to problem solve). (p. 28)

The problem lies not with surface learning, per se, but rather with failing to move students into deeper literacy learning.

But how?

By equipping them with the tools and affording them the opportunity to do so. In this chapter, we will highlight some of the types of teaching that will help provide students with these tools:

- Concept mapping
- Discussion and questioning
- Metacognitive strategies, including feedback to the learner
- Reciprocal teaching

We will also profile close reading, an instructional routine designed to foster deep learning.

Deep Acquisition and Deep Consolidation

As with surface learning, deep learning is divided into two periods: deep acquisition and deep consolidation. While the intention of surface learning is to expose students to and embed knowledge, the goal of deep learning is to foster self-regulation and self-talk. These two behaviors are critical for anyone moving toward greater expertise. You might recall an athletic endeavor you undertook in your own life. Doug was a competitive swimmer, but didn't turn into one overnight. His early swimming experiences were much like those of others. He took lessons as a child, learned different strokes, and so on. But the transition from recreational to competitive swimmer required more than simply extending the length of the lessons. He had to put the swimming skills he possessed to use in authentic ways by gaining experiences that showed him what he was capable of doing. A long swim in a crop irrigation canal showed him that he had the endurance, but the mild case of hypothermia and dehydration he contracted as a result taught him that what he knew wasn't sufficient. He joined a swim team, worked with some talented coaches, and learned from his teammates. The self-regulation, strategic thinking, and self-talk he acquired in the process were useful when he had to rise before dawn to go to practice, or forego attending a party with friends because of a swim meet the next morning.

> While the intention of surface learning is to expose students to and embed knowledge, the goal of deep learning is to foster self-regulation and self-talk.

Like other complex skills, students need opportunities to acquire and consolidate the use of these, in similar fashion to the acquisition and consolidation of knowledge discussed in the previous chapter. In the case of deep acquiring, students are learning how to plan, organize, elaborate, and reflect. They further consolidate through self-talk and self-questioning, both of which are necessary to becoming increasingly aware of their own metacognition.

Literacy learning goes part and parcel with the goals of deepening learning. Students need to talk about and listen to the ideas of others, especially those ideas that challenge their own current thinking. Students consolidate their conceptual understanding by writing. (We can't tell you how often we have figured out something through the act of writing.) They link concepts, values, beliefs, and ideas through the acts of reading and viewing—but only if their teachers expect this as an outcome.

Classroom discussion can just as easily devolve into the familiar Initiate-Respond-Evaluate (Cazden, 1988) model of interrogation. Doug calls it "Guess what's in the teacher's brain":

Teacher: What is the atomic number of nitrogen?

Student: 8.

Teacher: Nope. Try again.

Likewise, reading can be reduced to answering the comprehension questions on a computer program, and writing can look much more like a summary of someone else's ideas than an exploration of how the author's thinking has influenced one's own. We get what we ask for, and when we fail to ask for deep learning, it is unlikely to emerge on its own.

Deep Acquisition of Literacy Learning Made Visible

The pedagogical goal during the deep acquisition period is for students to assimilate knowledge, especially through integration with existing knowledge. This isn't merely an additive process. It's also subtractive, in the sense that new understanding may not jibe with previously held positions. The cognitive dissonance that results from being confronted by two contradictory ideas can be uncomfortable, and in that search for meaning, the learner has to make some decisions about how he or she will restore consistency. There's a higher degree of self-regulation that needs to take place, as students need to wrestle with ideas and concepts.

"My job is to make you comfortable with being uncomfortable," said ninth-grade English teacher Heather Anderson to her students at the beginning of the school year. "That's why it is so important that we have discussions about ideas, even those that you don't agree with. I want you to grow in your ability to think critically, investigate claims, and use reasoning and logic to examine issues. I won't tell you what to think, but I hope I show you where to look." This is when errors should be not merely tolerated but welcomed; this is where getting into the pit of not knowing is fun and powerful.

Ms. Anderson is signaling her expectation that her students will deepen their own learning. She understands that knowledge doesn't ultimately count for much of anything if it doesn't spark inquiry and resolve problems. Wiggins (1989) calls them intellectual virtues:

- Knowing how to listen to someone who knows something you don't know

- Perceiving which questions to ask to clarify an idea's meaning or value

- Being open and respectful enough to imagine that a new and strange idea is worth paying attention to

- Being inclined to ask questions about pat statements hiding assumptions or confusions (p. 48)

A critical difference between experienced and expert teachers lies in their ability to move students from surface to deep learning. John and his colleagues compared the practices and artifacts of teachers who had earned National Board Certification (NBC) with those of teachers who had applied for, but did not receive, this designation (Smith, Baker, Hattie, & Bond, 2008). The assignments were telling: 74% of the NBC teachers' work samples focused on deep learning, while only 29% of the non-NBC teachers' work samples evidenced deep student learning. In other words, the experienced but nonexpert teachers devoted far more attention to surface learning at the expense of deep understanding. More recently, researchers at the Education Trust (2015) reported similar findings. They analyzed thousands of middle school literacy assignments over a two-week period in spring 2015, and compared them to the Common Core State Standards, known for their intention to deepen student learning. The literacy analysis framework used by the researchers was organized in four domains:

1. **Alignment with the Common Core** such that it is grade level, and is clearly articulated to students

2. **Centrality of text** such that students are required to interpret and critically respond to texts using evidence

3. **Cognitive challenge** such that students are required to think critically and engage in extended writing

4. **Motivation and engagement** such that relevance and student choice are featured, allowing students to link to their goals

Only 5% of the assignments fell into the high range, leading the researchers to describe most of the assignments as "window dressing the Common Core" (Education Trust, 2015, p. 8). They reported that only 38% were aligned to the correct grade level, only 16% required textual evidence, and 85% focused on recall and reproduction of knowledge, rather than analysis, justification, and critiques. Slightly more than half (51%) of the assignments were completed in 15 minutes or less, thus thwarting extended writing, and only 2% offered meaningful choice and relevance.

Of course, simply telling students that they will engage in inquiry, investigation, and problem solving isn't sufficient if they don't have the time and tools to do so. That's why these researchers examined assignments, rather than teachers in the act of teaching, noting that assignments "reflect what teachers believe students can do independently as a result of their teaching" (Education Trust, 2015, p. 3). In order to assimilate knowledge during this deep acquisition period, students should be interacting with the curriculum and one another as they plan, organize, and elaborate on concepts. Much of this is fueled through concept mapping, discussions, and methods for conducting investigations. These are enacted through the literacies of reading, writing, speaking, and listening.

Concept Mapping

Concept maps and graphic organizers are visual representations of the relationships between and among ideas. Unfortunately, they are too often reduced to the level of worksheets, with the goal being to fill them out correctly, rather than to see one's thinking develop on paper or screen. It's transformation, not replication, that's key. Used well, concept maps and graphic organizers afford students the chance to take real ownership with texts and concepts, because they equip them with a tool for succinct summarization and visualization.

But key to using concept mapping well is to see it as an intermediate step to something else. In other words, what will students do with the graphic organizer once they've completed it? Most often, we use them to support extended writing and discussion of ideas. These are ultimately planning tools, and are frequently used during the prewriting process as students begin to outline their ideas and develop an organizational structure to follow (Flanagan & Bouck, 2015).

As with so many other instructional strategies outlined in this book, timing plays an important role. Moore and Readence (1984) reviewed studies on the use of graphic organizers, noting that those that were completed and presented to students in advance of a reading had a relatively small effect (0.08). However, those that were constructed by students after reading text were much higher (0.57), and students processed and rehearsed information differently. More recently, Swanson et al. (2014) found that the use of graphic organizers with students with learning disabilities positively impacted their comprehension of social studies texts. Their meta-analysis examined several literacy instructional practices, advising that "educators should embrace instructional practices and materials that support the facilitation of activating *what was already learned*" (p. 179; emphasis added). In other words, the greater effect was found in aiding students to deepen their knowledge, rather than in acquiring initial knowledge.

EFFECT SIZE FOR CONCEPT MAPPING = 0.60

The use of concept maps has a high effect size, but as always, it's the story behind the numbers that really matters. Concept mapping is effective when it is used as a planning tool for something else. If its use is limited to filling it out and then setting it aside, it is no longer effective. The power of a concept map comes from the cognitive work it prompts as students lay out a schema of what they know. Their planning—for writing, research, investigation, or presentation—is what makes it so useful.

Dahlia Negroponte uses word concept maps with her students to focus them on the terms that are most vital for them to know. Her class was reading *The Giver* (Lowry, 1993), a novel about a young boy growing up in a society where crime and fear have been eliminated. Ms. Negroponte knows that the concept of utopia is central to the novel's message, and one that is not easily understood by her sixth graders. She initially introduced the term to them at the introduction, and asked them to return to it periodically as they read and discussed the novel over a two-week period.

"They first learned the denotative meaning of the word, which is the start," she said. "I wanted them to gain a deeper understanding of the complexities of a utopian society as they followed Jonas's struggle to fit in."

The word concept maps provide her with a way to measure her impact, and she used Emir's as an example (see Figure 3.1 on the next page).

"I watched the evolution of his thinking as he read, wrote, and discussed the novel. His initial thinking is the definition. He wrote, 'It's a place where everything is perfect,' and as an example 'It's the place where Jonas lives.' But look at the evolution of his understanding over the first week." She pointed to his notes that moved from comparing utopia to a diamond, to likening it to a "room where if you move something, it's wrecked." Ms. Negroponte said, "Emir is beginning to see, like the character in the novel, that utopia can't be sustained, and he says that 'no place can be perfect forever.' That's a lot of wisdom coming from an 11-year-old."

Ms. Negroponte noted that the concept map was used again in an essay the students wrote about utopia after they had finished the novel. "They used their annotated notes and concept maps like these to write about whether a utopian society was desirable, and at what cost."

While this was only one of several concept maps students developed during the unit, she noted that their deepening understanding of the

WORD MAP

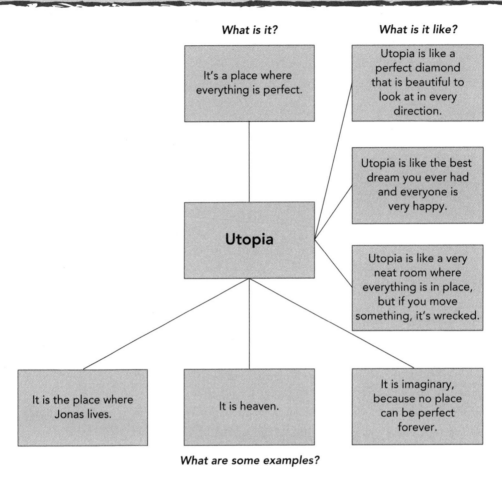

What is it?

It's a place where everything is perfect.

What is it like?

Utopia is like a perfect diamond that is beautiful to look at in every direction.

Utopia is like the best dream you ever had and everyone is very happy.

Utopia

Utopia is like a very neat room where everything is in place, but if you move something, it's wrecked.

It is the place where Jonas lives.

It is heaven.

It is imaginary, because no place can be perfect forever.

What are some examples?

Figure 3.1

term is evidenced in the evolution of their notes. "We use analogies to understand complicated terms by asking what it's like, and we build it out with examples. But what I like most is when we hang around these really nebulous terms like *utopia*. They're not easily defined and exemplified. It pushes their thinking quite a bit further," she said. "They understand why this novel is described as *dystopian*."

Discussion and Questioning

We've chosen to place discussion and questioning in the same section because we believe that effective teacher and student questioning fosters quality talk in the classroom. This is different from the Initiate-Respond-Evaluate method of recitation and interrogation, where the teacher asks the questions, evaluates the response given by the student, and then asks another question (Cazden, 1988). The IRE pattern encourages recitation of the text, but fails to deepen student thinking beyond the surface. Although there is widespread agreement that discussion is vital to comprehension and critical thinking, the implementation is less than robust. Nystrand's (2006) observations of middle and high school English classes found that the average length of whole class discussions varied from 14 to 52 *seconds* per period—hardly enough time for anyone to deepen his or her knowledge.

The evidence suggests that the students who benefit most from classroom discussion are those who are struggling to comprehend text, although why is not clear. Could it be that discussion allows for students to co-construct knowledge, in that the ideas introduced by one member spark understanding in another? Are classroom discussions effective because they heighten the level of student engagement with the text? Is it the value in noticing that other people think differently than we do (Wilkinson & Nelson, 2013)? We think about the professional and personal book clubs we've been involved in over the years. In every case, each of these dynamics was present at one time or another.

But just because students are talking more doesn't mean that it automatically results in deeper learning. There are some quality indicators related to solid discussion (Fisher & Frey, 2014). Students need to know the rules of discussion, both in small groups and as a whole class, as well as procedures for doing both. One of the expectations for students in Grades 3–5 is that they learn how to yield and gain the floor. But to do so means that the teacher needs to redefine his or her role in the discussion. By this age, children have learned that they need to raise their hand and be called on before speaking. Yet this can result in stilted conversation, and the teacher becomes the air-traffic controller. There

> Although there is widespread agreement that discussion is vital to comprehension and critical thinking, the implementation is less than robust.

> EFFECT SIZE FOR CLASSROOM DISCUSSION = 0.82

are certainly times when this is necessary, but we argue that true discussion occurs when students get to talk to one another without the teacher always being the intermediary.

Fourth-grade teacher Paula Taber changes the environment when extended whole class discussion occurs. The class has been reading *The One and Only Ivan* (Applegate, 2011), and the students are meeting to discuss a chapter of the novel they have just finished. She asks them to slide their chairs to the outer perimeter of the room so they can see one another, and she takes a seat as well. Ms. Taber poses discussion questions meant to provoke thought, and keeps a clipboard with her to track students' responses. She reminds them that each of them has up to five opportunities to contribute, but no more than that.

"One of our classroom norms is to share the air," she said, "so that we don't have a handful of people dominating the conversation. And remember, you can ask questions as well."

With text in hand, she asks her students open-ended questions, occasionally redirecting their attention to one another, not her. "Don't look at me for an answer. The answer's going to be right here in the room," she tells them. As the discussion continues, she asks a student who has already spoken several times, "Amal, you've spoken four times, but you only have one more opportunity. Do you want to use it now or save it?"

Students often opt to reserve their last comment in case they have more to say later. Ms. Taber also invites those who have not participated. "Jocelyn, we've only heard from you once so far, and we need your thoughts, too. How do you respond to Nathan's suggestion about the television set in Ivan's cage?"

Small group discussion is also essential as students delve more deeply into the texts they are reading. These discussions are not directed by the teacher, but instead are regulated by the students themselves. Usefulness discussion should allow students to engage in argumentation as they justify their positions and listen to the reasoning of others (Almasi, 1994). We call it "disagreeing but not being disagreeable."

> We argue that true discussion occurs when students get to talk to one another without the teacher always being the intermediary.

The students in Maria Tejeda's third-grade class used their argumentation skills as they discussed life cycles. One group was disagreeing about the differences between unique aspects of an organism's life cycle and aspects that all organisms have in common. They used their argumentation skills to discuss their ideas:

Sumaya: I think that they all have to be born. That's one thing that all of them have. Can we put that here? [pointing to the graphic organizer section focused on common aspects of life cycles]

Oscar: I agree with you because every one that we studied so far has been born alive.

Jason: I agree with you, too. I also think that they all have babies.

Oscar: I disagree with you 'cause I don't think that the bean seed has babies. Look at the pictures of the life cycle. There's no babies.

Sumaya: I agree with Jason because the plant can reproduce. It says right here [reading from their text]. But I don't think it means that they have babies.

Jason: You're right. I mean that they all reproduce. That's what I mean. That's the right word, not that they have babies.

Discussion is further strengthened when learners know how to mark the conversation, using statements that promote cohesion of ideas. These conversation markers include the following (Michaels, O'Connor, Hall, & Resnick, 2010):

- "Can you tell us more about that?"
- "Can you show me where you found that information?"
- "I agree with _____ because _____."
- "That's a great point."
- "I want to add on to what _____ just said."

Fifth-grade teacher Hector Ortiz provides students with table tents with each of the conversational markers listed and defined. Students practice these moves as a whole class and know that they are expected to use these markers when they work collaboratively. For example, in their book club conversations about *Petey* (Mikaelsen, 1998), the students integrate the moves.

David: Did everyone hear that? Sarah was reminding us about the doctor calling him an idiot.

Sarah: Where can we find that quote? I know we marked it in the text because we talked about it a lot. It was in the beginning of the book.

Jeffrey: I found it. It's on page 5. And then it says, "The child has no capacity whatsoever for even minimal sensory appreciation," and I wrote a note that says that he wouldn't understand anything from his eyes, ears, nose, or touch. Can anyone talk more about it?

Anna: Yeah, I remember that we talked with Mr. Ortiz about that. It seems so wrong that the doctors told Petey's mom that he was feebleminded, that he would never learn anything. But how does that connect with where we are now?

Sarah: I was just saying that we're seeing Petey has intelligence and that he's making decisions. The doctor was wrong, telling his parents that he couldn't do anything.

Their conversation continued with members of the group providing support for their peers and the discussion they had. As Mr. Ortiz noted, "Before I taught my students about accountable talk, their group conversations were limited and mostly focused on literal levels of thinking. Now, they know how to interrogate ideas without hurting feelings. It builds their relationships and the trust in our classroom."

EFFECT SIZE FOR QUESTIONING = 0.48

Teacher questioning frames these whole class and small group discussions. The questions asked can limit thinking, as is the case when teachers ask narrow questions with only one response. On the other hand, teachers can invite further speculation by changing the nature of the question to prompt more discussion. The first are funneling questions, in that they intentionally send students down a cognitive path with a known end point. Funneling questions have their place, especially in the surface acquisition period. But deepening understanding through discussion requires a focusing question approach (Wood, 1998). Consider the likely responses that would follow the funneling examples, and compare your predictions to those that focus student thinking:

- **Funneling:** What was the setting of the story?
- **Focusing:** How did the setting influence the story?
- **Funneling:** What is the meaning of the word *confusing*?
- **Focusing:** Why do you believe the author chose the word *confusing* in this passage?

When students are initially grappling with a complex piece of text, the questions teachers pose are frequently funneling questions. That's because students need a solid foundation of literal-level understanding about what's happening in the text. But after this initial phase of questioning, we want to deepen students' understanding through the type of focusing questions that get them to notice the structural and inferential dimensions of the reading. We describe four phases of text-dependent questions (Fisher, Frey, Anderson, & Thayre, 2015):

- What does the text say? (Literal)
- How does the text work? (Structural)
- What does the text mean? (Inferential)
- What does the text inspire you to do? (Interpretive)

These questioning phases are designed to systematically deepen a learner's understanding of a text, and discussion lies at the heart of close reading. We'll say more about the details of close reading later in this chapter, but for the moment we'll attend to the role of text-dependent questions that focus, rather than funnel.

Marcus Brown used this questioning pattern when he engaged in close reading and discussion with his seventh-grade students about "The Tell-Tale Heart" (Poe, 1843). After spending time at the literal level to

Video 3.2
Questioning for
Surface, Deep, and
Transfer Learning

*http://resources.corwin.com/
VL-Literacy*

ensure that his students were grounded in the foundations of the text, he turned his attention to the second phase—how does the text work?

To do so, Mr. Brown selected questions about the vocabulary in the text, and how it affected the meaning, asking, "What words and phrases does Poe repeat, and how does it affect the tone?"

He turned the students' attention to the author's craft, asking about how the punctuation used by Poe increases the anxiety felt by the reader. Each of these questions was marked by several minutes of extended debate and discussion as students began to notice things they had missed in earlier readings.

Later in the same lesson, Mr. Brown transitioned to the third phase of text-dependent questioning, "What does the text mean?" Here, he asked them about imagery, and the students drew back on their earlier observation that a watch was mentioned several times.

"All that ticking! It's like a heartbeat!" said D'Andre.

"Can a watch symbolize anything else?" asked Mr. Brown.

Now Elvira added, "Like time, of course. But you mean more, right, Mr. Brown?"

The teacher nodded and said, "It sounds to me like you're on the verge of something, Elvira. I want to give you a moment, because I'd like to hear more."

After a few moments, her eyes widened. "Like, I kept thinking about *watch* as a noun. But it can be a verb. Like he's being watched. And that's why he's so freaked out!"

Now Franco was intrigued. "Elvira, do you mean someone was really watching him? Because I didn't see that."

"Elvira, say more," Mr. Brown said, and she added, "No, he wasn't really being watched. But you know that creepy feeling when you feel like someone's watching you? That's what I mean."

D'Andre added almost simultaneously, "You feel that way when you're doing something you're not supposed to, and you might get caught. Like all jumpy and everything."

Mr. Brown smiled at this exchange because it was evidence that the discussion was leading to a deeper sense of meaning. "I'm pleased about where this is going. D'Andre, you made an important point about the narrator's mental state. So my next question is this: This story was written more than 170 years ago. What can you infer about the attitude toward mental illness at the time this was written, and what's your evidence?"

Close Reading

The practice of close reading, an instructional technique for inspecting a brief passage of text to determine its inferential meaning, is not a new one. Its history dates back to the 1920s, when New Criticism was on the rise as a means for interpreting texts at the word and sentence levels, as well as the entire passage (Richards, 1929). Close reading for many decades was the domain of college professors and advanced high school English teachers, and the works analyzed were primarily literary texts and poems. What is new about close reading is the application of many of these ideas in elementary and middle school classrooms (Fisher & Frey, 2012, 2014). This instructional routine combines several of the strategies profiled in this book:

- Students engage in **repeated reading** of a short passage to build fluency and deepen understanding.

- Students **annotate text** to mark their thinking.

- The teacher guides discussion and analysis through **questioning**.

- Students engage in extended **discussion** and analysis with their teacher.

EFFECT SIZE FOR REPEATED READING PROGRAMS = 0.67

EFFECT SIZE FOR STUDY SKILLS = 0.63

Close reading varies according to developmental factors related to reading. Emergent and beginning readers in the primary grades are read to, rather than reading independently. This is because the texts used during close reading are aligned more closely to their listening comprehension, rather than their ability to decode. The gap between children's listening and reading comprehension is substantial, and doesn't close until the end of middle school (Stricht & James, 1984). Close reading in primary is a time when the unconstrained skills of vocabulary and comprehension are foregrounded, and decoding instruction takes a backseat.

As students move to Grade 3 and beyond, they assume responsibility of performing the initial reading on their own. Many have worried that this will place struggling readers in harm's way, but keep in mind that in close reading students are reading and discussing the text many times. It's a form of slow reading, where the end game is not about volume, but rather about depth of understanding. The teacher pauses frequently to ask text-dependent questions that cause readers to look back into the text (and thus reread). These are focusing rather than funneling questions, and move from literal to structural and inferential levels of analysis. Because close reading is cognitively demanding, lessons are often extended over two or three sessions.

In the previous section, we profiled a portion of a middle school English teacher's close reading, but we didn't say anything about the fourth level: *what does the text inspire you to do?*

Kindergarten teacher Josué Paredes used the text *The Day the Crayons Quit* (Daywalt, 2013). For those of you who haven't yet had the pleasure of reading this, the story concerns a group of crayons who feel they have been treated unfairly and decide to go on strike. Each has written a letter to Duncan, the young boy who owns them. For example, purple crayon doesn't like the fact that Duncan uses him carelessly and colors outside the lines, and peach crayon won't come out of the box because Duncan has peeled off his wrapper. When it came time for Mr. Paredes's students to move into this fourth phase, the majority of students chose to write about the book. But others selected different routes. Several children wanted to find out if the author wrote any other books, and visited his home page (with help from the teacher). Two boys were intrigued about the dispute yellow crayon and orange crayon got into regarding which was the proper color of the sun. The boys searched Google Images and saved images to sort into either orange or yellow. And one enterprising student chose to write her own set of letters, this time from her shoes. In her letters, some never got worn, others had to work on holidays, and a pair of flip-flops didn't like getting wet all the time.

Our point in telling you about this is this: students need teachers who give them the time, opportunities, and tools to deepen their knowledge. Mr. Paredes understands that if students are going to deepen their knowledge, he needs to plan for it. Many of these events involve investigation, writing, and performance. As they move into deep consolidation, they benefit from approaches that foster metacognition, self-talk, and the ability to examine texts outside the direct guidance of the teacher.

> Deep consolidation approaches foster metacognition, self-talk, and the ability to examine texts outside the direct guidance of the teacher.

Deep Consolidation of Literacy Learning Made Visible

As students deepen their knowledge, they also need the time and tools to consolidate their deep learning. In this period, students are conducting investigations, reading additional materials, and working with peers to make sense of complex texts. They depend on metacognitive thinking and self-regulation as they progress toward this increasingly self-directed learning. Metacognition is the ability to think about and reflect on one's learning (Flavell, 1979). This is where students are taught to be strategic in their planning, thinking, and learning. The process is both a learned one, as students build the habit of reflective thinking, and a developmental one, as they progress toward more abstract thinking. A comparison of the discussions held with a child and an adolescent certainly makes this apparent. Although a youngster has fewer tools (language, cognition) to explain her motives behind a transgression, a teen is going to be able to do so, even if she's not going to tell you. The ability to think more metacognitively begins around age 3 and develops into adulthood (Kuhn, 2000), and is further enhanced through strategies that build habits of reflection, and by feedback that illuminates when strategies work and when they do not.

The conversations and discussions adults have with children can foster or inhibit thinking. For example, asking students, "What are you learning?" rather than "What are you doing?" gets them to attend to the purpose of the task at hand, rather than the activity itself. Asking students to "tell me what you understand so far" builds the expectation that they should be monitoring their learning. This last one is of particular value at the deep consolidation phase as it sets up the kind of student questioning you need to assess your own impact and make further instructional decisions. It's almost impossible to ask a question about something you know nothing about; that isn't the case with students in this learning period. They know quite a bit, and can craft their next questions to you based on what they currently understand. Even more so, students should pose questions for themselves. Self-questioning plays an important role in monitoring one's reading comprehension (e.g., Johnson & Keier, 2011). A reader who monitors her comprehension of the text is also going to recognize when she has lost the thread of meaning.

In the next section, we will discuss the value of comprehension strategy instruction to foster metacognition, self-questioning, and self-regulation. Students moving into deep consolidation are increasingly driving their own learning, and these thinking practices keep them moving forward. We don't mean to suggest that students are working independently, with little guidance from the teacher. Literacy practices that foster such application include reciprocal teaching because it requires students to mobilize specific behaviors while engaging with complex texts as well as their peers. All the while, the teacher is providing feedback that models the kind of self-talk we want our students to be able to furnish for themselves. The deeper learning phase is a critical time for students to apply these approaches to their learning.

Metacognitive Strategies

Metacognitive awareness is vital to the learning process, and specifically to reading and writing. Palincsar (2013) describes metacognitive awareness as consisting of three parts:

1. Knowledge about our learning selves

2. An understanding of what the task demands and necessary strategies to complete them

3. The means to monitor learning and self-regulate

In other words, it describes our ability to observe our own thinking. But students need guidance in how to become more metacognitively aware. A collection of approaches, outlined in the pages that follow, is designed to teach students how to plan tasks, monitor comprehension, and evaluate their progress.

> EFFECT SIZE FOR METACOGNITIVE STRATEGIES = 0.69

Self-Questioning

As a person reads or views something, he or she is monitoring comprehension. This is not a fully conscious realization, but rather one that runs just under the narrative he or she is taking in. We'll use a detective story as an example, because it is one so many are familiar with. As you are reading or viewing the story, you are tracking the plot, analyzing characters, noticing when the setting changes, and querying the spoken and hidden motives of all of the characters. At the same time, you are on alert for clues that might appear that will allow you to solve the crime. If something occurs to disrupt your understanding of these elements, you will probably either go back a few pages to reread, or pause the video to ask the person next to you, "What just happened?" Running in the background is a well-attuned method of self-questioning, as you continually ask yourself, "Does this make sense?" and if it doesn't, "What do I need to do to regain understanding?"

Humans are pattern-seekers and meaning-makers, and we continually strive to make sense of what is happening around us. When it comes to reading, there exists an innate need to make sense of text. But readers also need to be taught how to monitor their comprehension, and what to do when it breaks down. This is accomplished through two approaches:

> EFFECT SIZE FOR SELF-VERBALIZATION AND SELF-QUESTIONING = 0.64

1. Provide questions readers can use as they query their understanding

2. Teach students to pause periodically throughout a text to generate their own questions

Provide Questions

Furnishing predetermined questions during the deep consolidation phase is useful as it reminds students about the metacognitive practices they need to propel their learning and monitor comprehension. It is common for students who are deep into a unit of study to engage in investigation and research. But the advent of online sources has introduced other considerations that teachers of earlier generations did not face. The Internet is an excellent source for digital material, but it is also fraught with problems that can derail student projects. Chief among them are issues of credibility and accuracy of information. Teachers aren't able to curate source materials as they once did, and now must equip students with the ability to question sources. Eighth-grade English teacher Kim Van Natta teaches students a method for critically analyzing Internet sources as they conduct investigations for extended writing. She posts these questions on every laptop in her classroom:

1. Does this site contain information that is accurate?
2. Does it identify the hosting institution?
3. When was it last updated?
4. Are there links to other sites? Are those links of similar quality?

The ultimate goal for her students is to be able to evaluate websites themselves, so that they can critically analyze information. "But I also know this takes years to develop, being able to use a critical and skeptical eye," said Ms. Van Natta.

To accomplish this, she has modeled and used a think-aloud approach to introduce them to the process, using a digital source critique sheet that accompanies their research (see Figure 3.2).

"I want them to be able to screen Internet sources, and I require them to submit these critiques as part of their bibliography. It's not enough to just cite the source. I want them to have looked at these sources closely."

Her intent, however, doesn't stop at getting her students to successfully complete forms. "This is a bridge to the kind of self-questioning habits

WEBSITE EVALUATION TOOL

URL: _____

1. Title of website: _____

2. What is the main purpose of the website?_____

   Is it selling something?   Does it describe a service?   Is it an educational site?

3. Who created the website? _____

   Is there a contact name? Is it a private company? Is it a school? Is it a government agency? Is there an "about us" section?

4. How current is the website? (When was it last updated?) _____

5. Are links available to other sites? (Try some of them to make sure they work.)

   _____

6. Are there references or citations? _____ If yes, what are they? _____

   _____

7. What new information did you learn from this website? _____

   _____

   _____

8. What information is missing? _____

   _____

   _____

Figure 3.2

 Template available for download at **http://resources.corwin.com/VL-Literacy**

they need when confronted with information," she explained. To do so, she embeds similar questions into discussions. "When I show them a video clip on a topic, for example, I ask them to critique what I have shown them," said Ms. Van Natta. "I feel that's a major responsibility of my job teaching adolescents. Can I build the habit of scrutinizing information closely? That's an intellectual habit that will stay with them long after they've left my classroom."

Teach Students to Ask Their Own Questions

A second method for fostering self-questioning is by creating points when they compose their own questions. This approach is particularly useful as students read longer pieces of narrative and informational texts. Many children adopt a naïve assumption that people read long passages without interruption, and then process all the information at once. Teaching them how to break a text into more manageable chunks so they can use self-generated questions will equip readers with strategies for maintaining understanding.

Fifth-grade teacher Joyce Gomez uses a method described by Berkeley, Marshak, Mastropieri, and Scruggs (2011) to build the habit of teaching her students to engage in self-questioning when working with informational texts. She uses headings and subheadings in articles and textbooks as stopping points for students to ask themselves questions.

"When we first began doing this at the beginning of the school year, I did lots of modeling, as you can imagine," she said. "I taught them about why self-questioning is important, and made note pages for them like this one to structure the process," she continued, displaying the sheet found in Figure 3.3. "As we've progressed, I have faded out the note pages and shifted them to writing questions in their journals. I leave it to them to chunk the text for themselves, because not everything we read has headings and subheadings."

Ms. Gomez speaks to individual students to check in with them about their self-questioning. "I ask them to answer a question they've written. If they can, I give them feedback about the use of this strategy. If they can't, I ask them about other strategies they can use to regain understanding."

SELF-QUESTIONING

Directions: Before reading, write down a question you expect to be answered in each section. At the end of each section, see if you can answer your question. If you can't, use one or more of these strategies to help yourself.

- Reread the passage with your question in mind.
- Check for unknown vocabulary (look inside and outside the word or phrase).
- Check graphs, diagrams, or photographs that are in the section.
- Write your question to ask me about it.

Article Title: "The Sun in Our Solar System"

Heading: The Sun Is a Star Your question:	Now that you have finished, can you answer your question? Yes No
Subheading: Our Sun and Other Stars Your question:	Now that you have finished, can you answer your question? Yes No
Heading: Features of the Sun Your question:	Now that you have finished, can you answer your question? Yes No
Subheading: Temperature and Composition Your question:	Now that you have finished, can you answer your question? Yes No
Subheading: Layers of the Sun Your question:	Now that you have finished, can you answer your question? Yes No

Figure 3.3

Template available for download at **http://resources.corwin.com/VL-Literacy**

Reciprocal Teaching

The emphasis in reciprocal teaching is on deploying comprehension strategies to make meaning, engaging in self-questioning, and chunking texts into smaller passages. All of this is done in the company of a small group of peers, who work together to co-construct meaning from text (Palincsar & Brown, 1984). The evidence of reciprocal teaching is broad: Palincsar (2013) notes that other researchers have found it to be effective with students with disabilities, English learners, and bilingual students. Although reciprocal teaching can be used in service of students acquiring a surface level of knowledge, the expression of so many features necessary for deepening learning made it a good candidate for this chapter.

Reciprocal teaching (RT) is a structured reading routine enacted by four students who are working through a piece of text. RT discussions are composed of four strategies, which are systematically introduced and taught:

- **Summarizing** each passage to extract key information and central themes

- **Questioning** at the literal, structural, and/or inferential levels about the passage

- **Clarifying** information and ideas through discussion and checking in with peers

- **Predicting** the content of the next passage, given what the author has explained thus far

The teacher segments the text into smaller chunks, and students are taught to pause after reading each segment to discuss its content using these four strategies. Because RT enlists so many complex cognitive behaviors, teachers commonly introduce it across multiple lessons, as each comprehension strategy is practiced and then paired with subsequent strategies until students are adept at doing all four. In the early stages when students are still learning about RT, they are typically assigned these as formal roles (summarizer, clarifier, and so on). But as Palincsar (2013) notes, the larger goal is that students deploy these strategies "opportunistically" (p. 370).

EFFECT SIZE
FOR RECIPROCAL
TEACHING = 0.74

Video 3.3
Reciprocal Teaching:
Predict and Question

*http://resources.corwin.com/
VL-Literacy*

Therefore, formal roles and structured dialogues give way to more organic discussions about complex text.

Holly Baker listens for this kind of discussion in her sixth-grade language arts classroom. The staff at her school adopted RT as a signature practice several years ago, which means that she doesn't have to spend much time on teaching the procedure. "The kids at the school have been using RT since third grade, so the only ones I need to teach it to are the ones who are brand new," she said. Because her students have had several years of experience in using RT to understand text, Ms. Baker is able to employ it almost immediately.

"We've been reading some informational articles about child labor laws to augment our focus on the working lives of boys and girls," she explained. She joined a group of four students who had located information about children who worked in the United States in the 19th century. The students were debating the implications of a passage about the number of children:

Grecia: It says in here that 18% of children had jobs in 1900.

Brandon: But you're missing something, because it also says that this was "understated." It says "at least" 18% had jobs, so maybe it's more.

Sarita: But how much more? I don't think there is a way to know that.

Grecia: I agree, because the author also said that there were lots of people coming to the U.S. . . .

Sarita: . . . and remember that the last section said that there wasn't a lot of enforcement of the child labor laws, so . . .

Kiara: I wrote it in my notes: "people looked the other way." So what changed?

Brandon: Maybe that's what's in the next section.

Ms. Baker later said, "I was glad to hear that level of discussion, and how they just talk about what they're reading very naturally. But it also gives me some insight into how to follow up with them. I'll find out what they're still wondering about at the end of the article, and help them figure out what they need to research next."

Feedback to the Learner

The metacognitive and self-regulatory skills of students are strengthened through feedback from the teacher. When the feedback is delivered such that it is timely, specific, understandable, and actionable, students assimilate the language used by the teacher into their own self-talk. What we say to children, as well as how we say it, contributes to their identity and sense of agency, as well as success. The messages that students receive externally become the messages they give themselves. We're speaking not strictly of praise, but rather of making sure that we not only commend learners when, and for what, they are doing well, but also label their actions for them. When a student needs direction, our feedback should assist her in identifying the actions she needs to take in order to get back on the path. Saying to a learner, "What can you do next to find that answer?" sends an underlying message that she has agency and can take steps. In contrast, telling a learner, "The answer is on page 37," without giving her an opportunity to resolve what's blocking her, tells her that you don't believe she is capable of doing so. Students shouldn't be reduced to tears in trying to move forward—we don't want to withhold information from students indefinitely—but we do want them to develop the kind of self-talk they need to persist when things get difficult, and to bounce back when confronted with failure.

It's important to say that we are not enamored with failure. No one likes to strive toward something only to repeatedly fall short of the goal. Having said that, small failures are a part of the learning process, and can actually lead to a more attenuated understanding of why something didn't work the first time, so as not to repeat it again. It's not the failure in isolation that we're talking about, but rather the pairing of a small failure followed by a small success.

Effective teachers look for opportunities to give feedback to students by playing back what occurred. Saying to a student, "I can see you had

EFFECT SIZE FOR FEEDBACK = 0.75

Video 3.4
Teacher Feedback That Labels Students' Actions

http://resources.corwin.com/ VL-Literacy

trouble with this part of the assignment, but then you solved it. What did you do that led to this success?" alerts him to think reflectively about the strategic thinking and action he took to get himself over a hurdle. In doing so, we give him the internal scripts he needs to become an increasingly self-directed learner.

It is equally important that we not dilute feedback with praise. Dweck (2006) has written extensively on the damage praise about the individual can do in reinforcing a fixed mindset, rather than a growth mindset. Students with a fixed mindset have been conditioned to believe that innate qualities such as intelligence and talent are the keys to success, and they discount the role of effort or their own agency. Although we don't mean to, too often we communicate our own beliefs in a fixed mindset when we tell students, "You're so good at reading!" instead of saying, "You're reading comprehension has really improved this quarter. Look at the difference in your scores since the last quarter. I've also seen how much more time you're spending each day in independent reading." Highlighting progress further builds a learner's sense of agency as he sees the relationship between his success and his actions.

Hattie (2012) speaks of three internal questions that drive learners:

- Where am I going? What are my goals?
- How am I going there? What progress is being made toward the goal?
- Where to next? What activities need to be undertaken next to make better progress? (p. 116)

The feedback we give students at any point in their learning falls into four levels:

- **Feedback About the Task:** How well has the task been performed; is it correct or incorrect? For example, "Your goal was to list all of the reasons why this event occurred so you can organize your essay, but the second point is unclear. You need to change the wording so that your argument is stated using an active voice, rather than a passive one."

> What we say to children, as well as how we say it, contributes to their identity and sense of agency, as well as success. The messages that students receive externally become the messages they give themselves.

- **Feedback About the Process:** What are the strategies needed to perform the task; are there alternative strategies that can be used? For instance, "I can see that you're not sure what categories you want to use for your concept word sort. What is another way you could solve the problem?"

- **Self-Regulatory Feedback:** What is the conditional knowledge and understanding needed to know what you're doing (self-monitoring, directing the processes and tasks)? For example, "When you got frustrated with your group, you moved your chair back and took a breather. Then you rejoined them a minute or two later, and your group completed the task. Why did that work for you? How were you different after you rejoined them?"

- **Feedback About Self:** Personal evaluation and affect about the learning. For example, "Excellent job! You are such a talented writer."

The first two levels, task and process, are more commonly used in classrooms, and we witness teachers using these on a frequent basis. The fourth level—feedback about self—is unfortunately used too often by well-meaning teachers. Although meant to bolster self-esteem, it appears to have a zero to negative impact on learning, especially in discouraging students from engaging in any further revision of their work (Hyland & Hyland, 2006). We want students to think positively about themselves, and praise is a tool that can contribute to positive teacher–student relationships. The message should not be interpreted as "do not give praise"; instead, the message is to separate the praise from feedback about the task, and the learning. It's important that adults don't withhold their unconditional positive regard for students, but praise that masquerades as feedback can undermine efforts to motivate and encourage.

But it is this third level of feedback—self-regulatory feedback—that plays such a prominent role during deep consolidation. Think about the instructional approaches we have profiled in this section. All of these methods offer critical opportunities for teachers to dialogue with students as they delve into increasingly self-directed learning. Consider the power of the self-regulatory feedback 11th-grade English teacher Brad Stevenson gave to a student who was having difficulty composing a literary critique of a novel she had read, using a psychoanalytic criticism frame:

Mr. Stevenson: When I talked with you yesterday, you weren't sure where you were going to go next in your literary criticism essay. What needs to change for you to get reenergized?

Shakira: I don't really like this frame, with all that business about Jung and Freud.

Mr. Stevenson: So it doesn't feel natural to you. If you were analyzing this story, what frame would you select?

Shakira: Well, a feminist slant makes a lot more sense to me. And the protagonist is a woman.

Mr. Stevenson: I can see why that makes sense, but I think you're overlooking the era it was written in. It was written when psychoanalytic thought was at its peak.

Shakira: True, but I just don't like it.

Mr. Stevenson: I want you to notice right now that it's feeling uncomfortable, and why it's feeling that way. Is it because it's stretching you?

Shakira: [laughing] Yeah, it is.

Mr. Stevenson: So recognize it's a stretch and a challenge, and remember that your goal at the beginning of this year was to broaden your understanding of world literature and formal criticism. What steps should you take next to get yourself better prepared for this assignment?

Shakira: I guess I need to go back to my notes and materials about psychoanalytic criticism.

Mr. Stevenson: That sounds like a good start. I admire how you're pushing through this, even though it's not your go-to lens for viewing this story. Let's talk tomorrow in class after you've done that studying you talked about. And I'll want to hear how that action has made you more confident about completing this assignment.

Throughout the conversation, the teacher kept the focus on feedback, not praise. Yet clearly this was a warm and encouraging conversation. He spoke about the task and the process, but really emphasized Shakira's ability to take action and change the outcomes. To be sure, the discussion took a few minutes to conduct. But the time is well worth it, and is critical as students move from deepening their learning to moving into transfer. Our efforts to equip students with the tools, strategies, and scripts for talking to themselves make moving to transfer, which is the subject of the next chapter, possible.

Conclusion

In order for students to deepen their knowledge, they need to have their learning made visible to them. It's how they can take action on what happens next. The language and behaviors we use with them assist them in understanding who they are as learners, what the task demands are, what strategies they can leverage to resolve problems, and how they can persist when things are difficult. Embedded within these is resiliency. Learners who are resilient can come back from failures and incorporate challenges into their growing sense of who they are. Consider anything you've learned and that you value as an accomplishment. Without a doubt, you faced challenges, and sometimes some failures, as you completed that journey. Now consider who guided you along the way. Chances are just as good that those people equipped you with tools and strategies to move forward, using language and behaviors that you took to heart. Teaching requires lots of heart, along with an unflagging belief in the ability of your students to achieve success. Don't be afraid to tell them, and show them, your confidence in them.

> Learners who are resilient can come back from failures and incorporate challenges into their growing sense of who they are.

TEACHING LITERACY
FOR TRANSFER

4

Most of us have rented a car at one time or another. Rarely is the one we rent the same make and model as the one we drive at home. Yet after a few minutes of orienting ourselves to operating the mirrors, adjusting the seat, and figuring out how to turn the headlights and windshield wipers on, we pull out of the parking lot and set forth. How are we able to operate a complicated piece of machinery in an unfamiliar location? Because we are able to transfer what we know about cars and driving to a new situation. Sousa (2011) uses this as an example of transfer of learning in action. The driving example works for you because you are engaged in a bit of transfer as you read this. There are several reasons why this example works, and they have everything to do with methods for promoting transfer of learning.

The first reason this works for you is because it is a situation nearly every adult has experienced, and is therefore immediately relatable. Even if you have not rented a car, you are able to relate this to borrowing a friend's car. A close association between a previously learned task and a novel situation is necessary for promoting transfer of learning. A second reason this works is because there is an analogy at play here, in this case comparing driving a car with complex learning. Analogies, metaphors, and similes are useful in encouraging students to identify patterns. But this falls apart if we use the driving example with someone who has never operated a car. A limiting factor in fostering transfer is in pairing the experience with the knowledge base of the learner. In the case of a nondriver, we would need to find a different example. If that person plays tennis, for example, he or she might be better equipped to transfer those skills to learning the game of racquetball. And that brings us to the third reason: knowing the learner developmentally and experientially is essential when promoting transfer of learning.

But there's one more factor, and perhaps the most critical one, and that is we have the skills to detect the similarities and differences from one situation to another. We know the key differences up front are the mirrors, seats, and headlights, and we know the key similarities are the brakes and accelerator. Having the skills to detect similarities and differences is a key skill to transfer—without it, we may transfer our driving skills from our old car and, whoops, an accident waiting to happen.

A close association between a previously learned task and a novel situation is necessary for promoting transfer of learning.

Moving From Deep Learning to Transfer

All of the work we do as teachers is for naught if students fail to appropriately transfer their learning. One of the concerns is that students (often struggling ones) transfer *without* detecting similarities and differences, and the transfer does not work (and they see this as evidence that they are dumb). Memorizing facts, passing tests, and moving on to the next grade level or course is not the true purpose of school, although sadly, many students think it is. School is a time to apprentice students into the act of becoming their own teachers. We want them to be self-directed, have the dispositions needed to formulate their own questions, and possess the tools to pursue them. In other words, as their own learning becomes visible to them, we want it to become the catalyst for continued learning, whether the teacher is present or not. However, we don't leave these things to chance. Literacy is a major engine in this process, as no matter how curious a child might be, his learning is limited by the constraints of his literacy skills. Therefore, we teach with intention, making sure that students acquire and consolidate the needed skills, processes, and metacognitive awareness that make self-directed learning possible. By showing students how we ourselves are learners, we in turn model for them how they can teach themselves. Figure 4.1 on the next page summarizes the relationship between what we do as teachers and how those teaching behaviors create the conditions for transferring learning.

Transfer is both a goal of learning and a mechanism for propelling learning. Transfer as a goal means that we want students to begin to take the reins of their own learning as they deepen their own knowledge. Transfer is also a mechanism for learning such that students acquire, consolidate, and deepen their knowledge as they move forward and continue to learn. In the next sections, we'll turn our attention to transfer mechanisms. When we have an understanding of how transfer occurs, we can better establish the conditions for ensuring that students meet transfer goals.

Types of Transfer: Near and Far

Transfer occurs throughout surface and deep learning. In fact, *all* learning is transfer, provided understanding is involved (Bransford,

Highly effective teachers . . .	Such that students . . .
Communicate clear learning intentions	Understand the learning intentions
Have challenging success criteria	Are challenged by the success criteria
Teach a range of learning strategies	Develop a range of learning strategies
Know when students are not progressing	Know when they are not progressing
Provide feedback	Seek feedback
Visibly learn themselves	Visibly teach themselves

Source: Hattie (n.d.).

Figure 4.1

Brown, & Cocking, 2000). By this, we mean that transfer is more than memorization; it also involves recognition on the part of the learner about what has occurred. It is more helpful to consider this across two dimensions: near transfer and far transfer (Perkins & Salomon, 1992).

Near transfer occurs when the novel situation is paired closely with a learned situation. For example, a young child who is learning sight words has been able to recognize these words in isolation on flash cards, but now can identify specific words in running text. Primary teachers recognize the significance of this leap as a time when the child is signaling that she is ready for more complex applications. But primary reading teachers will also ask the child how she knew those words, in an effort to prompt recognition through metacognitive awareness. Kindergarten teacher Ina Tano'na asks, "You read that sentence smoothly. I'm curious about this word. You said it was *where*, and you were right. Where have you seen that word before?" When Mina answers, "It's on my iPad" or points to the word wall in the classroom, Ms. Tano'na knows that the student is moving from memorization to near transfer.

The size of the leap is larger in *far transfer*, as the learner is able to make connections between more seemingly remote situations. For example, when Mina is able to consistently and correctly use *where* in her original writing, she has moved to far transfer. Again, primary teachers aren't surprised at all about this trajectory of learning, and in fact teach sight words through multiple modalities, including seeing, saying, defining, and writing the word to promote this transfer. And that's exactly our point— Ms. Tano'na knew exactly where she wanted Mina to go in her learning, and she taught accordingly to foster both near and far transfer of learning.

The Paths for Transfer: Low-Road Hugging and High-Road Bridging

So far we have discussed transfer across a continuum from near to far, with the novel situations becoming increasingly remote. However, they remain conceptually similar to one another. Now let's introduce mechanisms, or paths, for transfer: low-road and high-road transfer (Perkins & Salomon, 1992). In this case, the contrastive element is the extent to which the thinking involved is under the learner's conscious direction. Figure 4.2 summarizes each of these mechanisms.

Mina's performance was due in part to the increasing automaticity she could draw upon in recognizing sight words in different situations—an example of *low-road transfer.* In other words, with growing automaticity came a corresponding decrease in the amount of conscious attention she needed. Her teacher employed a hugging technique by creating these low-road opportunities that stayed close to the original target, allowing Mina to see the similarities of sight words across print. But soon the teacher moved from hugging to a *high-road bridging* technique as she increasingly challenged Mina to generalize concepts, including spelling and writing the word in isolation, and later within sentences. It is likely that her ability to use *where* when writing an original story may have also required some conscious self-direction about strategies. She may have checked her spelling against the example on the word wall, or read her sentence aloud to herself to see if it made sense, and then

> Knowing the learner developmentally and experientially is essential when promoting transfer of learning.

HUGGING AND BRIDGING METHODS FOR LOW-ROAD AND HIGH-ROAD TRANSFER

Hugging to Promote Low-Road Transfer *Students are learning to apply skills and knowledge.*	Bridging to Promote High-Road Transfer *Students are learning to make links across concepts.*
The teacher is associating prior knowledge with new knowledge.	Students are using analogies and metaphors to illustrate connections across disciplines or content.
Students are categorizing information.	Students are deriving rules and principles based on examples.
The teacher is modeling and thinking aloud.	Students are thinking metacognitively and reflectively to plan and organize.
Students are summarizing and rehearsing knowledge.	Students are creating new and original content.
The teacher creates role-play and simulation opportunities for students to apply new knowledge to parallel situations.	Students are applying new knowledge to dissimilar situations.

Figure 4.2

compared it to the story she was developing to see if it fit. In this case, she is also employing some high-road transfer as she reminds herself to use the early writing strategies Ms. Tano'na has been teaching her. In the process, Mina's literacy learning is becoming more visible to her. In those moments, she is taking command of her own learning as she teaches herself.

We intentionally used a kindergarten example to illustrate transfer because we want to ensure that it is understood that transfer as a mechanism (1) occurs even among the youngest learners and (2) changes in appearance as the learner progresses developmentally. If we had started with an example of a high school student, it might have been misunderstood as something that only happens with older learners. So now let's look at evidence of different types of transfer, and the use of different paths of transfer, with an adolescent in mind.

Ninth-grade student Sara Edwards is enrolled in English, and the first unit of study involves understanding the heroic cycle in literature. This is a foundational theory in understanding narratives in Western literature, and it will be a concept her English teacher, Jonas Kennedy, will return to throughout the year. Over a two-week period, Sara learns about the heroic cycle, initially through terminology and simple examples, such as identifying elements in familiar childhood stories like "The Lion King" and the Harry Potter series. Mr. Kennedy knows that his students are of an age where they have seen or read these stories and can recall their details, with some occasional support using short clips that isolate actions. Sara's learning is mostly *near transfer* of surface learning early on, as her teacher has intentionally selected visual and written text excerpts that are familiar to his students, a *low-road hugging* technique. In addition, the teacher has done much of the conceptualization for them, in that he has selected texts where the heroic cycle is very much in evidence. As the unit progresses, he frequently reviews the elements of the heroic cycle so that Sara and her classmates are able to assimilate knowledge of the stages, such as separation, descent, ascent, and unification. In time, Sara is able to recall these with increasing automaticity, thus freeing up cognitive space to attend to the more conceptually demanding task of analyzing texts.

Mr. Kennedy is also upping the challenge in terms of the texts they are reading and discussing. The texts are getting more complex, and the heroic elements are not as clearly in evidence. Sara reads short stories like "The Interlopers" by Saki, looking for elements of the hero's journey, as well as those that do not neatly fit this pattern. Soon she and her classmates are exploring antiheroes, and Sara is now comparing and contrasting these concepts with texts such as *Fahrenheit 451* by Ray Bradbury (1953). Her learning is deepening as her teacher uses more *high-road bridging* techniques to foster increasingly conceptual thinking.

Mr. Kennedy is leading Sara and her classmates on a journey that begins with near transfer as she initially associates new knowledge (the heroic cycle) with familiar stories. Early in the unit, he read grade-level texts where the heroic cycle is clearly in evidence, and over time transitions to far transfer as students evaluate similarities and differences across

All learning is transfer, provided understanding is involved.

texts. The English teacher introduces formal literary theory, as Sara reads excerpts from Joseph Campbell's *The Hero With a Thousand Faces* (1949). By the end of the first quarter, Sara and her peers are engaged in Socratic seminars on heroes and antiheroes in literature and in contemporary society. Sara links the efforts of candidates in a current election campaign to cast their life stories as ones similar to those in the heroic cycle, demonstrating a high-road transfer as she draws associations from two seemingly disparate sources. Importantly, Sara's learning has become visible to her, as she transforms knowledge consciously and with intention. At these times, she has become her own teacher.

Thus far, we've presented transfer in discrete categories, but in practice, it is not so clear-cut. In other words, there is a continuum between near and far, and between hugging the low road and bridging to the high road. Transfer is what makes it possible for students to acquire and consolidate the surface learning that is foundational for deep learning. As students deepen their learning, we look for them to think in increasingly conceptual ways. We want them to move from declarative knowledge (what it is), to procedural knowledge (how to use it), to conditional knowledge (when to use it) (Paris, Lipson, & Wixson, 1983). In the remainder of this chapter, we'll highlight ways to promote transfer toward conceptual learning. Transfer is the conduit, and we can intentionally instruct to cultivate it. This requires establishing the conditions that make it possible, and using bridging high-road transfer practices that make it probable.

> We want students to move from declarative knowledge (what it is), to procedural knowledge (how to use it), to conditional knowledge (when to use it).

Setting the Conditions for Transfer of Learning

It should come as no surprise that a major condition for transfer to occur concerns relevancy. Learning becomes more meaningful when learners see what they're learning as being meaningful in their own lives. Relevancy doesn't have to be at the world peace level, but it does need to have implications that are developmentally appropriate and are seen as being useful in students' learning lives. Those learning intentions and success criteria that we discussed at length in Chapters 1 and 2 are just as important for promoting transfer as they are for fostering initial learning. Although students are engaged in more self-directed learning during this transfer period, they need goals and ways to measure their own progress. Earlier in this book, we talked about how problem-based learning is not effective during surface learning, in large part because students haven't acquired and consolidated the knowledge they need to even begin to analyze and create. But as students deepen their knowledge, introducing them to a problem is a great way to promote transfer by building relevance into what they do.

Middle school teachers Janice O'Reilly, Marcus Stevens, and Alice Leong collaborated on an interdisciplinary robotics unit for the seventh graders they teach. The teachers' instructional intentions were to teach their students about using literacies to investigate and then design a robot that could perform a simple task. Math teacher Mr. Stevens taught the students about calculating rate and distance of objects, while science teacher Ms. O'Reilly led the students through processes to build their coding skills. English teacher Ms. Leong taught her students principles of conducting online research and working as a team to communicate effectively, establish goals, develop a timeline, and set deadlines. These are vital as students become their own teachers, because learners need to be able to identify goals and know when they have been successful. "This has been more difficult for them to do than I would have predicted," said Ms. Leong. "They've been conditioned that goals are imposed on them by adults."

Importantly, the problem of programming a robot was not the initial focus of instruction for any of the teachers. Instead, each sought to lay down a solid foundation of knowledge and skills. "We used to be in a hurry to introduce the problem right at the start," said Ms. Leong. "But when we started analyzing the impact of our unit, we realized that lots of kids weren't learning much. And with so much work on our part!" she said. Now the team waits to introduce the problem until after they have evidence that the students possess enough knowledge to move forward. Only then are design teams formed so that they can apply what they have learned. This is consistent with Hattie's (2012) caution that "merely learning to enquire without embedding that enquiry in a rich basis of ideas is not a defensible strategy" (p. 95).

Video 4.1
Teaching for Transfer

http://resources.corwin.com/ VL-Literacy

"These teams need to be able to code, to do the math needed, and to work with one another, if they're going to be successful," said the English teacher. "They can't be learning all of these things while they're trying to design a robotic task. It's like changing the tires on a bus while it's moving." As the teams begin to take charge of their learning, the teachers are able to observe closely and receive feedback from students about what is needed. "Because of student feedback, I've improved the online research instruction I've been giving," said the English teacher. "The relevance is definitely there," she noted, "but without the knowledge and skills, and lots of feedback going in both directions, this project can't be a success." She admitted that her favorite project this year was one designed by a team to transport the teacher's coffee cup across the classroom floor.

The conditions created by these middle school teachers allow for teams to think conceptually, especially in identifying problems and proposing solutions, testing their proposals, making adjustments, and thinking of alternatives, all dispositions identified by Bereiter (2002) as evidence of transfer of learning.

Younger children can do this as well, and it needs to be centered on not a problem, per se, but rather a project. Third-grade teacher Yolanda Freeman uses digital storytelling as a way of causing students to integrate visual and written literacy skills and digital communication tools. However, she understands that writing is diminished when students don't have an audience in mind. Like many educators, she collaborates with other teachers around the world so that students can write to and for one another. Each student in her class is paired with someone in another third-grade class—this year, it's a class in a town just north of Toronto, Canada. Students Skype with one another to share ideas—a challenge with the time zones. "It's a three-hour difference, so the Canadian teacher and I are always figuring out schedules," she said. However, these live sessions are vital for the student writers, as they "move from conversation to composition" (Bereiter & Scardamalia, 1982, p. 1).

The children share their ideas and question each other about the narrative or informational text they are developing; then each works independently. Once they have a draft version, they upload it to a shared site.

"Here's what's most important about these projects," Ms. Freeman said, "and it's how I've made a major shift in my teaching. I used to do projects one time, and then move on. But this is a major transfer skill for my students to accomplish. They are learning to communicate across different platforms, with a variety of people, using multimedia. So we do these projects throughout the year, with different partners in the Canadian class."

The students in both classes learn about preproduction, production, and postproduction elements, including planning and storyboarding. The tasks change as the year progresses. The first project of the year is "Tell Me a Story," which requires students to convey a real or imaginary experience. The second is a bit more complex. It is titled "Teach Me Something," and their shared purpose is to inform and explain. In addition, this project requires that students incorporate animation techniques rather than still images. The third project focuses on critical literacy, and includes tasks related to "Making Responsible Choices," "Whose Story Isn't Being Told?," "A Worthy Cause," and "Taking Action."

"This is where we spend most of the year," said Ms. Freeman. "And this is when I really see the transfer to those critical thinking skills we want to see." She notes that these last projects, which occur every month, require students to persuade using evidence. "I'm teaching about using evidence in writing in class, of course, but having a clear idea about who your audience is makes all of this so much more relevant."

Teaching Students to Organize Conceptual Knowledge

To think more conceptually, students need to figure out how the surface knowledge they have acquired to understand concepts, and the deep knowledge they have developed about how ideas relate to one another, comes more fully under their own command. In large part, students benefit from organizing conceptual knowledge so they can analyze their understanding and identify where they need to go next in their learning. Importantly, it is the student who is in the driver's seat.

EFFECT SIZE
FOR ORGANIZING
CONCEPTUAL
KNOWLEDGE = 0.85

Students Identify Analogies

In the previous chapter, we wrote about the use of analogies and metaphors for teaching about the structures of concepts and the way that they can be related to other similarly structured concepts—for example, relating plant and animal cell structures to a factory, where each part has a specialized function. These analogies work like "coat hangers" in a closet, as new knowledge is draped onto an existing form, and can be easily retrieved later (Hattie, 2012, p. 102). As students move to transfer, teachers are looking for them to locate analogous information in how they explain concepts. This may not happen spontaneously, but can be part of the expectations for how students explain and share information.

Analogies are effective when they are aligned with the experiences of the audience. To do so requires that students understand their audience, in order to identify the right analogy or metaphor that will work. Reading specialist Mona Adam works with struggling middle school readers. Part of the students' work is in developing reading lessons to use with the first-grade students they tutor. Cross-age peer tutoring involves older students teaching younger ones, and has been effective with developing the literacy skills of the older tutors (Jacobson et al., 2001). Ms. Adam's students write literacy lesson plans to implement weekly with their "reading buddies," including word work, reading a story, and writing a response. The reading specialist has taught these tutors about the effectiveness of analogies, which is featured in each lesson plan.

"I ask them to find a comparison or a similarity to something else. Something their reading buddies will probably already know," she said. "It really causes them to have to take on the perspective of a younger child." Ms. Adam has used lots of examples to build their skills, such as finding synonyms and antonyms for unfamiliar words, as well as descriptive analogies that show a characteristic. Derek, a struggling reader himself, designed a lesson for his reading buddy using the picture book *What Do You Do With a Tail Like This?* by Steve Jenkins (2003). The book features parts of animals, and the reader is to identify what animal each might belong to. Derek developed analogies that focused on the function of the body part to use in his read-aloud to his first-grade buddy. He wrote sticky notes to himself and posted them on the pages:

- Elephant's trunk is like a garden hose that can spray water.

- Platypus's nose bill is like a shovel for digging.

- Alligator's nostrils are above the water, like a snorkel for breathing the air.

- Giraffe's tail is like a fly swatter.

"I'm pleased, of course, about Derek's literacy development, in terms of planning discussion and writing notes to himself to organize his lesson," said Ms. Adam. "But I am especially happy to see him and other students thinking critically about how they can use analogies and metaphors to compare and contrast information. I hear it in their discussions as well, like when we're talking about a text and someone asks, 'What's a good analogy we could use here?'"

Peer Tutoring

While we're on the subject, we will explore the field of peer tutoring more completely. A number of meta-analyses have been performed on the effects of peer tutoring programs on the achievement, self-concepts, and attitudes of tutors and tutees (e.g., Ginsburg-Block, Rohrbeck, & Fantuzzo, 2006). Peer tutoring programs work best, and the effect is as high on the person doing the tutoring as on the person being tutored

EFFECT SIZE
FOR PEER
TUTORING = 0.55

- When they are structured

- When tutors have received training

- When the tutor and tutee are of different ages

Ms. Adam's cross-age peer tutoring program introduced in the previous section describes these conditions. However, teachers have witnessed similar effects in their own classrooms, too, as one peer works with another to learn something new. It is important to say that peer tutoring should not be about always positioning a high-achieving student as the tutor who is aiding a low-achieving peer. The effectiveness of this approach includes partnerships that are the reverse.

Lonnie Pelletier uses peer tutoring in his fifth-grade classroom routinely. All of the students in his classroom are English learners, and they speak a variety of native languages. Once a week, he partners students according to their language levels, pairing students with differing levels of language proficiency together. "The critical factor isn't whether they both share a native language. It's that one student is one proficiency level ahead of the other," he said. He explains that he does this so the gap isn't too large between the partners. He taught all of his students how to support the learning of the other, and each student takes the role of being a coach, and being a reader. "I use the PALS method for supporting each other's reading," the teacher explained. These Peer-Assisted Learning Strategies (Fuchs, Fuchs, Mathes, & Simmons, 1997) include reading a text aloud to one another and retelling it, locating the main idea, and making predictions about the next section. Student pairs also use coaching statements to help each other by

Video 4.2
Peer Tutoring

http://resources.corwin.com/ VL-Literacy

- Pointing to a miscued work and telling their partner to check it

- Providing clues when their partner is stuck or isn't able to answer a question

- Reminding their partner to "shrink it" if he or she explains the main idea in more than 10 words

- Prompting their partner to make a prediction based on what was read

- Writing the statements of their partner so that they can be discussed

After one partner has served as the reader and the other as a coach, the roles are reversed. Using a new but conceptually related text, they repeat the process. For instance, Mr. Pelletier had his students read two short informational texts on shark conservation efforts. The partners unpacked vocabulary for one another, worked on pronunciations, and took dictation so that they could see how their oral language was being transformed into written form. After both pieces of text were read and discussed, the partners then composed at least two investigation questions they still had.

"The next day, the partners work together again to conduct some online research the readings prompted. I collect their questions and then curate some websites in advance so the searches are a bit more contained, but I like what I see happening," he said.

On Friday, the fifth-grade teacher assembles them in a circle, and the students tell one another about their investigation questions and what they found. "They are becoming more confident in their own language learning, and they look for feedback from one another. But what I like best is that they are getting into the habit of asking questions and then acting on them," said Mr. Pelletier.

Reading Across Documents

Mr. Pelletier is capitalizing on another method for facilitating transfer of learning by having students read, investigate, and write across multiple documents. Many students become adept over time at summarizing the information in a single text, identifying its main arguments, and reporting on key details. But this becomes much more challenging when reading across texts, especially when those texts contain conflicting points of view. The ability to adopt a critical approach to analyzing multiple texts is a mark of a student who is thinking conceptually. On the other hand, those who accept textual information at face value, without questioning its source or seeking corroboration, are at risk for not transferring knowledge. A study of undergraduates who were confronted with multiple documents containing conflicting information about the possible health risks associated with cell phones found that those with a simplistic view of knowledge (i.e., an accumulation of facts) had difficulty processing across texts (Ferguson, Bråten, & Strømsø, 2012). However, those who understood that doubt and seeking resolution are vital to knowledge building fared much better. In other words, students who held a mental model of how one builds knowledge that included questioning, doubting, investigating, and seeking resolution were able

> The ability to adopt a critical approach to analyzing multiple texts is a mark of a student who is thinking conceptually.

to understand the arguments in the text at a deeper level than those who viewed learning as fact-gathering.

To be sure, those mental models take a lifetime to build, as anyone who has ever had to weigh the merits of smartphone data plans can attest. But teachers can deliberately create such opportunities for their students and provide them with the feedback and coaching they need to wrestle with multiple texts. Middle school English teacher Robyn Artiles and life sciences teacher Jim Hawthorne collaborated with one another to create this dissonance without alerting their students ahead of time. At the same time that Mr. Hawthorne was teaching about the benefits of scientific methods for animal testing in laboratories to ensure product safety, Ms. Artiles had her students reading policy papers and government bills designed to eliminate the practice. Their students were left in the uncomfortable position of sense making when two respected teachers had seemingly disparate ideas about animal testing. When one student finally confessed to his English teacher that he didn't know what to believe, she did not divulge the intent of the unit of study (to promote critical analysis of a controversial scientific topic), but rather invited him and the rest of the class to engage in a deeper investigation.

Problem-Solving Teaching

In Chapter 2, we noted that our challenge as educators is not to just identify what works, as almost everything works for some students at some time, especially when zero growth is expected. Rather, we need to match what works to *accelerate* student learning, and then implement it at the right time (Hattie, 2009). Problem-based learning is one such practice. The evidence is that when PBL is used early in the learning cycle, before students have had sufficient experience with learning the declarative and procedural knowledge needed, the effect size is very low: 0.15. This is surface-level knowledge, and they just aren't equipped with enough knowledge to pursue inquiry. But when problem-solving *teaching* is employed, the effect size skyrockets. Unlike conventional PBL, where the problem is presented to students in advance of knowledge acquisition, problem-solving teaching is deployed when students are already deepening their knowledge. That is just what the English and life sciences teachers did.

Video 4.3
Reading Across Documents Collaboratively With Teacher Feedback

http://resources.corwin.com/ VL-Literacy

EFFECT SIZE FOR PROBLEM-SOLVING TEACHING = 0.61

Confronted with conflicting information, the eighth graders in Ms. Artiles and Mr. Hawthorne's class were issued a challenge by their teachers: investigate the issue more thoroughly and craft an argument that supports your position. The students had previously learned about Aristotle's persuasive techniques of *ethos* (credibility), *pathos* (an emotional appeal), and *logos* (appeal through reasoning) in their English class. As well, they were grounded in the scientific method, and had experienced this form of reasoning countless times in their science classes.

Both teachers reminded students about these forms of argumentation and reasoning, and that a position can't be supported using only one pathway. Over several days, students conducted independent investigations, and then met to form teams for a debate in support of or in opposition to the issue. The science teacher formulated the proposition:

> Animal testing is necessary for research, and must be preserved using legal and ethical principles.

As Burek and Losos (2014) note, "Similar to a trial, the debate opens and closes with the burden of proof on the proposition" (p. 50). The teachers use the Middle School Public Debate Program, designed by Shuster and Meany (2005). Ms. Artiles's students had previously used this debate format and were familiar with it, albeit using topics she had selected for them. The format of the debate is as follows with each student responsible for a single two-minute speech:

- First Proposition Constructive speaker
- First Opposition speaker
- Second Proposition Constructive speaker
- Second Opposition speaker
- Opposition Rebuttal speaker
- Proposition Rebuttal speaker

The remainder of the students had conducted research, collaborated to construct arguments, and rehearsed their speeches. On the day of the debate, a panel of judges, including the principal, a parent, and several members of the school faculty, scored the arguments, while Ms. Artiles and Mr. Hawthorne served as coaches for the two teams. While Mr. Hawthorne's proposition team was judged to be the winner of the debate, both teachers knew that all of their students had won.

"We've conducted debates for several years, but we realized we were giving them the topic without them having any idea where they stood," said Mr. Hawthorne.

The English teacher added, "By waiting until they had already begun formulating positions, there was an authentic reason to hold the debate. Instead of lethargic kids dragging around, we had students who had their own need to answer these tough questions," said Ms. Artiles. "They're learning to think for themselves, and not because someone told them what to think."

Teaching Students to Transform Conceptual Knowledge

As students transfer their learning at the conceptual level, they learn *when* to use the knowledge they have or are pursuing. This conditional or strategic use of knowledge quickens the pace of the learning, and as such, the line between organizing and transforming conceptual knowledge is blurred. For example, the middle school debaters moved rapidly back and forth as they organized and transformed knowledge about scientific animal testing. This is true learning at its best, as students oscillate among surface, deep, and transfer learning, made all the easier as they deepen their understanding of a concept. Keep in mind that knowledge begets knowledge, and one of the strongest predictors of a learner's future capacity to learn is what he or she already knows (Murphy & Alexander, 2002). Debates, such as the one described at the end of the previous section, suggest how seamlessly students can move from organizing to transforming knowledge. Additional literacy learning opportunities listed in this section can furnish students with the forums they need as they become their own self-directed teachers.

EFFECT SIZE FOR
TRANSFORMING
CONCEPTUAL
KNOWLEDGE = 0.85

Socratic Seminar

Long used in advanced classes as a means for provoking critical thinking, Socratic seminars have enjoyed more recent success with elementary learners as well. Unlike a debate, in which two clearly opposing arguments are weighed against one another, the purpose of a Socratic seminar is for members to help one another understand a text deeply by linking it to other ideas and values. It draws on many elements of discussion and thinking discussed elsewhere in this book, including accountable talk, rules of discussion, and metacognitive thinking. Close reading of a text occurs in advance of the Socratic seminar. Israel (2002), writing for the National Council of Teachers of English, defines the Socratic seminar as

> a formal discussion, based on a text, in which the leader asks open-ended questions. Within the context of the discussion, students listen closely to the comments of others, thinking critically for themselves, and articulate their own thoughts and their responses to the thoughts of others. They learn to work cooperatively and to question intelligently and civilly. (p. 89)

Although named for Socrates, these sessions do not cleave to the tradition of Socratic method, where the goal is to unearth an underlying truth. In traditional Socratic discussion, the questions posed by the leader are designed to funnel the members toward a predetermined truth. Therefore, the questions are more often closed-ended and somewhat leading (Schmit, 2002). However, in classroom Socratic seminars, the questions are open-ended, and "the objective . . . is exploration rather than discovery" (p. 73). When students are first learning how to engage in a Socratic seminar, the discussion leader is the teacher, who develops open-ended questions in advance of the meeting. Students sit in a circle with the text in hand, and address one another as they question the text and each other.

As a group of learners becomes more proficient with Socratic seminars, students are encouraged to become discussion leaders, and the teacher becomes another participant. This is the case in Franco Williamson's

As students transfer their learning at the conceptual level, they learn *when* to use the knowledge they have or are pursuing.

sophomore English class. During a unit on immigration stories, the students asked to circle up in an impromptu Socratic seminar so they could discuss an article they had read by Anna Quindlen titled "Love, Hate Still Stew in the New Melting Pot" (1986). Students in the class disagreed with one another about whether the text reflected current tensions and opportunities in their community, or whether it should be considered part of a past that is no longer relevant. Noah and Dulce, whose parents had emigrated respectively from Somalia and Guatemala, volunteered to lead the discussion. Their discussion questions included these:

- What types of people live in the narrator's neighborhood, and how does it differ from our own experiences?

- Why does the tone of the text shift? What does this say about her?

- What kinds of situations unite Quindlen's neighbors? What does this say about human nature? Is this our experience?

Over the course of 30 minutes, the students dove deeper into the text. On one occasion, Mr. Williamson had to remind students that the goal of the seminar was not to persuade one another, but rather to figure out the deeper meaning of the text. From time to time, he posed follow-up questions to encourage a student to supply evidence or expand on his or her thinking, but for the most part, Noah and Dulce led the discussion. When the Socratic seminar came to a close, Mr. Williamson asked his class to engage in a freewriting session for 15 minutes. "Your goal is to get 200 words down on paper, while these ideas are still fresh in your minds. Consider the meaningful links you're making to other texts you've read in this class or elsewhere. We'll pick this up tomorrow."

Extended Writing

Writing is the result of knowledge construction. Evidence of a student's transfer of knowledge can be found in the extended writing pieces he or she creates. Writing instruction, like reading, is a constellation of approaches, as students move from ideas (surface), to thinking (deep), to constructing knowledge (transfer). While the effect size overall for writing programs is a decent 0.44, understand that this covers quite a bit of territory. Embedded within effective writing instruction is teaching students to summarize as part of their study skills and engage in careful planning by mapping concepts. As such, young students learn about writing processes initially as a series of discrete steps, but should move quickly into the thinking that is required of writers as they plan, organize, and revise their original writing. Writing instruction is also a constellation of effective teaching practices. The feedback loop between the teacher and peers is critical as students immersed in writing seek and offer feedback from others. And don't overlook the importance of a writer's understanding of the goal. Like other elements of learning, writers benefit from clear learning intentions and success criteria related to the audience, the purpose, and the format (Graham & Perin, 2007). In other words, the way that writing is taught and guided makes a significant difference in how well students are able to use this as an expression of their construction of knowledge.

Mr. Williamson, the 10th-grade English teacher, understands that his students' ability to transfer knowledge is predicated on reading and discussing complex texts, especially as students interrogate concepts and link these to other texts and schools of thought.

"Writing isn't solely about turning in an assignment on the due date," he says. "Writing should be a means to uncover one's own thinking in the process."

He challenged students to link the ideas presented in Quindlen and either support or argue against her assertions about the metaphor of the melting pot as an American ideal. One student drew on a work studied early in the year, G. K. Chesterton's "The Fallacy of Success" (1915/2004), to support his claim that the myth of the "industrious apprentice" persists in American popular mythology. Several students used Quindlen's later work, especially her essay "A Quilt of a Country" (2001), written 10 years after "Melting Pot," to trace how her own thinking shifted in the wake of a terrorist attack. Still another cited a series of radio interviews with writers Junot Diaz, Jhumpa Lahiri, and Joseph O'Neill on the challenges, unfulfilled promises, and individual successes as immigrants

EFFECT SIZE FOR WRITING PROGRAMS = **0.44**

EFFECT SIZE FOR TEACHING STUDENTS TO SUMMARIZE = **0.63**

EFFECT SIZE FOR CONCEPT MAPPING = **0.60**

EFFECT SIZE FOR FEEDBACK = **0.75**

EFFECT SIZE FOR TEACHER CLARITY = **0.75**

Video 4.4
Providing Teacher and Peer Feedback

http://resources.corwin.com/ VL-Literacy

to raise important questions about the lure of the tropes we use tell our own stories.

"We've spent significant time exploring the use of the literary devices of tropes, especially metaphors, allegories, irony, and synecdoche," Mr. Williamson said. "It made me happy to see her weaving these concepts together."

Embedded within effective writing instruction is teaching students to summarize as part of their study skills and engage in careful planning by mapping concepts.

While the end products were impressive, they didn't begin that way. Mr. Williamson teaches his students about the role of critique and feedback in writing. From the first week of school, students receive direct instruction about giving feedback to one another, as well as how critiques are used by these writers in revision.

"I have lots of students every year who are under the impression that revision means simply making the corrections that came from editing," said the teacher. "I show them how you incorporate feedback and critiques into the next draft, and the next draft after that. I show them the feedback on my writing I get from my own editor, and how I use it to revise."

Before they submit their final draft, he asks them to compare it with earlier versions of the paper, and explain the revisions they made. "This is where I get the early buy-in from them, because they see how weak their first drafts were in comparison to the place they end up." As for his terminology—*final draft?* "Any writer will tell you you're never really done. You just run out of time," he smiled.

Time to Investigate and Produce

We were originally going to call this Genius Hour, as many educators have adopted the approach popularized by Google in which engineers are given a significant percentage of the workweek (up to 20%) in order to pursue their own projects. Also called Makers Ed, students are encouraged to devote time to investigating and developing their knowledge about topics such as science, technology, engineering, the arts, and mathematics (STEAM). We've been energized by being in the presence of young people who are working with purpose as they experiment with ideas. We've seen students building robots: one set of enterprising sixth graders sent a small robot carrying a note to the principal that said, "Please come to room 103. Emergency!"

The principal said it took about three minutes to get there. "Good thing it wasn't a real emergency," he chuckled.

In a kindergarten class, we watched students take daily photographs of the pea plants on their classroom windowsill, then convert them with a little adult help into a stop-action video so they could see how they grew. They then wanted to know the answer to the question, "Why do plants die?" which led to a whole new round of Genius Hour projects as students worked to find the answer. These are solid examples of students transferring knowledge through production.

But like conventional PBL approaches, students are not going to benefit from opportunities to research and investigate their own problems and questions if they don't have a solid foundation of knowledge to use as a springboard for their investigations. Notably, Google's lauded investment in creativity is directed at its highly accomplished engineering staff who already possess deep wells of knowledge to draw from. It's not likely that you'll get the same effect from simply announcing that every Thursday afternoon is dedicated to an hour of being a genius. Structure, of course, is essential. You can't just turn students loose without some procedures in place and expect that everything will be fine. On the other hand, we shudder at the bloom of "Genius Hour worksheets" that seem to be gaining popularity.

Opportunities for, and expectations of, transfer of knowledge should be woven into classroom life. We understand that setting aside sacred time to devote to this is appealing, and plausible. However, nothing magical happens at 1:30 p.m. if there hasn't been preparation. Students should be continually challenged to develop projects and investigations across the learning day. Asking students, "How could you use this?" near the end of a lesson can spur the kind of metacognitive thinking essential to learning. "How will you know you are successful?" reminds students (and ourselves) that one's internal measure is as important as an external evaluation.

Educator Angela Maier notes that investigation and production aren't moments in time, but rather should be part of the learning climate of the classroom. Like the mind frames for teachers we discussed in Chapter 1 that speak to a set of actionable values, Maier's "12 most genius questions" cultivate curiosity and channel how classroom time is utilized to extend learning:

1. How can we make it/each other better?

2. How do we know this to be so?

3. Is this what is needed most?

4. What is it we hope to accomplish, and what's stopping us?

5. What are we most proud of?

6. What is possible?

7. When can we start?

8. How will we prevent failure?

9. Who can/how can we make this happen?

10. What do we regret most?

11. How can we make the best use of . . . ?

12. What if we . . . ? (Dream big!)

Source: http://www.angelamaiers.com/2012/03/12-most-genius-questions-in-the-world, © 2011

Time to investigate is not of much use if it doesn't lead to production. We've witnessed this too many times during independent reading and writing times. While the majority of the students get down to business pretty quickly, there's often a few who listlessly flip the pages of a book, or gaze off into space, their paper or screen distressingly blank. When asked what they're doing, they reply indignantly, "I'm thinking!" Mind you, thinking is good. But without expectations about production, some students will not avail themselves of these opportunities to become their own teachers.

Fifth-grade teacher Melinda Jeffries, like many teachers, dedicates time each week for students to engage in investigation and production. "It's true that we have a 90-minute dedicated block of time to do this," she said, "but the preparation lasts the entire week."

Ms. Jeffries meets regularly with students to discuss what they're curious about, then helps them formulate a proposal for the time. "They'll usually start with some vague topic, like 'pollution' or 'cars.' I get them to move from a topic to a problem."

For instance, Sallahudein expressed interest in cars. With his teacher's help, he narrowed the focus of investigation to learning about how car engines worked "because a big problem is how to run cars without using gasoline." His initial investigation was on learning about traditional car engines, and how they are different from those that run on alternative fuels.

"Each week, the students give each other a quick update about their project, the problem, what they learned, and what they still don't know," Ms. Jeffries said. "This keeps them mindful of the processes they're using to resolve this dilemma."

The product is just as important. "I didn't suggest that he design an engine," she said. "But we did collaborate to figure out what his measure of success was going to be."

Sallahudein decided that he needed to be more knowledgeable about why alternative fuel engines are limited in range, and why they're so expensive. "I've seen a Tesla, and they're really cool, but why do they cost so much?"

His teacher continued to challenge him on this. "Why do you need to know that?" she asked.

"My friends and I talk about them, but none of us really understands them," he replied.

"So you need to be able to talk knowledgably about them," she said. "How would you know you could do that?"

Within minutes, Sallahudein had an idea. "I could meet with my friends who are in this class in a few weeks and explain what I've learned, and they could ask me questions. They might ask me questions I don't know the answer to, but then I can find out more."

Sallahudein is using all the literacies to learn: reading, writing, speaking, listening, and viewing. He's conducting web searches, reading blogs, writing notes, summarizing what he's learned, and organizing information so his friends will understand. The literacies themselves are running in the background, while his curiosity about the subject is more overtly directing his learning. Ms. Jeffries is a coach for him and the other students, teaching them about locating keywords to refine his searches, and partnering with him to figure out a digital system for him to capture his notes to himself.

"What's helpful to me is that when we're learning some of these skills during other parts of the day, like in the reading and language arts block, I can make connections to what the children are investigating. It's more than me knowing the topics they're interested in. I'm right there with them when they get themselves stuck, and then unstuck. It's thrilling when they see success moments after they thought they were doomed."

Conclusion

"I am a change agent."

This isn't a platitude. In the hands of an effective teacher, visible teaching and learning center our practices. It's true that some students will engage in transfer learning without any of us paying much attention to it, but that signals a lost opportunity as well. The keyword in the first sentence is *agent*. As teachers, we have the potential for tremendous agency—to make learning happen—if we'd only seize the chance to do so. Being a change agent means bearing witness to student learning, reflecting on it, and recognizing that student progress tells us something about ourselves. How will we ever know what students are truly capable of if we don't get deeply involved in their learning lives?

This last question has implications for assessment, which is the subject of the next chapter. As we have written before, a staggering majority of what is assessed requires surface-level knowledge, thus reinforcing to students that we only care about factual and declarative knowledge. But it's really difficult to assess for deep and transfer learning if we rarely witness it occurring. How can we assess students when we don't really know the limits of what they can achieve?

DETERMINING IMPACT, RESPONDING WHEN THE IMPACT IS INSUFFICIENT, AND KNOWING WHAT DOES NOT WORK

5

"How was the lesson?" asks Maria Ramirez of her teaching partner Shawna Branson. "Oh, it was great. Really great! The students really liked it. They seemed to pay attention the whole time, and they liked the video clip that we found."

We're pleased to hear that students enjoyed the lesson and that they paid attention. It's important that students experience joy at school. And attention is a necessary condition for learning. But we expect more. Lessons should impact students' learning. It's insufficient to simply say that a lesson was good (or bad) and that students liked it (or didn't). As educators, we should know the impact learning situations we create have on students. In fact, we believe that it is teachers' professional responsibility to determine how the lessons they develop and deliver impact students' learning. Thus far in this book, we have focused on what works best to accelerate learning from a research perspective. Putting each of the approaches we've discussed into practice is likely to ensure better learning, especially when specific strategies are linked with the specific phase of learning students need. But we don't leave this to chance or make the assumption that there will be an impact. We test it. We evaluate it. And when the desired impact is not achieved, effective teachers take action.

> We believe that it is teachers' professional responsibility to determine how the lessons they develop and deliver impact students' learning.

Determining Impact

Way back in Chapter 1, we discussed effect sizes. As you probably recall, an effect size is a quantitative measure of the strength of a phenomenon. In other words, it tells us how powerful something is in creating change. And, as you probably recall, an effect size of 0.40 (calculated with Cohen's *d*) indicates that, on average, the student(s) gained a year's worth of growth for a year in school. The implication is that 0.40 should be the expectation for instruction and intervention. An effect size of *less* than 0.40 suggests that the instruction or intervention was less than effective and may warrant change or revision. At the very minimum, an effect size below 0.40 begs for a discussion about the effort.

The effect size tool can be applied at the classroom level as well. Teachers can calculate effect sizes for their classes and individual students to determine the impact their instruction and intervention have had. This builds teachers' sense of efficacy, which is the belief in their ability to positively impact student learning. Jerald (2007) noted that teachers with strong self-efficacy

- Tend to exhibit greater levels of planning and organization

- Are more open to new ideas and are more willing to experiment with new methods to better meet the needs of their students

- Are more persistent and resilient when things do not go smoothly

- Are less critical of students when they make errors

- Are less inclined to refer a difficult student to special education (Protheroe, 2008, p. 43)

Over time, as teachers discuss the data and success with their peers, they develop collective teacher efficacy. Goddard, Hoy, and Hoy (2000) define collective teacher efficacy as "the perceptions of teachers in a school that the efforts of the faculty as a whole will have a positive effect on students" (p. 480), with teachers agreeing that "teachers in this school can get through to the most difficult students" (p. 480). Importantly, perceptions are formed based on our experiences. When teachers experience success collaborating with peers and those collaborations improve teaching and learning, they notice. These accumulated data points become the collective efficacy researchers note is powerful (Hoy, Sweetland, & Smith, 2002). We're just saying that the definition of success, on which these perceptions and thus collective teacher efficacy are built, should include student learning.

> EFFECT SIZE FOR COLLECTIVE TEACHER EFFICACY = **1.57**

Student learning at the classroom level can be held to the same standard as researchers, an effect size of at least 0.40. The process of calculating an effect size is fairly simple. Before we discuss that, it's important to remember a few things:

1. **Lessons should have clear learning intentions.** It's hard to determine whether students have learned something if they (and we) aren't sure what it was they were supposed to learn.

An effect size tells us how powerful something is in creating change.

2. **Lessons should have clear success criteria.** The success criteria provide the tools necessary to assess learning. If the success criteria involve writing about history, then learning has to involve both writing and content-area learning. Sometimes teachers conflate success criteria and are unable to determine if students have learned something, even when they have.

3. **The success criteria indicate what quality looks like.** To determine whether or not learning has occurred, students and teachers have to know what success looks like. As Collins (2001) noted, good is the enemy of great. If students believe that good enough is sufficient, they may only reach for that level. When they understand what excellent work looks like, they can reach higher.

4. **Students should know where they stand in relation to the criteria for success.** When students have no idea if they've done well or not, learning is compromised. Students should understand that learning is on a continuum, that errors are opportunities to learn, and that they can learn more.

With these four conditions in place, teachers are ready to examine the impact of the learning experience.

Preassessment

It starts with a preassessment, the first key part to evaluating progress. Without a preassessment, we cannot determine if learning occurred. When teachers only use postassessments, such as end-of-unit tests, essays, or projects, they will know who has demonstrated the expected level of achievement (and who has not), but they won't know who has learned because learning is a measure of change over time.

It's easy to overlook the preassessment and accept achievement as learning. But without it, becoming a better teacher and designer of amazing learning situations is left to chance. For example, Gina Humphrey assessed her kindergarteners during the first week of November on their letter recognition, which is a worthwhile literacy skill. Students should recognize the letters of the alphabet, both lower- and uppercase. Ms. Humphrey

Video 5.1
Visible Literacy Through Success Criteria

http://resources.corwin.com/ VL-Literacy

noted that all but four of her students could name the letters of the alphabet. That was their current achievement. It didn't tell her anything about the impact of her teaching or the lessons she designed on their learning because she did not have a baseline. What if the majority of the class had attended a transitional kindergarten class and already knew all of their letters in September? In that case, the time Ms. Humphrey devoted to learning letters was a waste. What if none of her students knew their letters at the onset of the year? In that case, the lessons were probably pretty powerful, and she might want to share the lessons with her grade-level team. This kindergarten example highlights a missing part of many teachers' instructional practices. Failing to identify what students know and can do at the outset of a unit of study blocks any ability to determine if learning has occurred and thus any ability for there to be a discussion about effective instruction and intervention.

Armed with baseline, preassessment information, teachers can design instructional interventions to close the gap between what students already know and what they are expected to learn. In this case, time is used more precisely because specific strategies can be selected based on the type of learning needed. Students who have a need for surface-level learning are probably not going to do well with a series of problem-based learning lessons. On the other hand, students who need deep consolidation learning are probably not going to benefit from learning mnemonics.

Postassessment

Once the lessons have been completed, teachers readminister the outcome measure. This opens the door to an investigation about impact. Did the lessons that were taught change students? That is learning.

When the pre- and posttest data are available, the effect size can be determined. As an example, Figure 5.1 contains the writing rubric scores from a middle school class. Brad Jacobs uses a 7-point rubric so that he can provide more precise information for students about their development. The rubric includes descriptors for the traits of writing, such as ideas, organization, word choice, sentence fluency, conventions, and presentation (e.g., Culham, 2010).

To calculate an effect size, first determine the average for the posttest and the average for the pretest. It's easy to do this in an Excel spreadsheet. Here's how:

- Type the students' names in one column.

- Type their scores for the pre- and postassessments in other columns.

- Highlight the column with the preassessment scores and select the "average" tool and place the average at the bottom of that column.

- Do the same for the postassessment column.

In the writing example, the average preassessment score was 3.74. After three months of work on understanding traits of writing, receiving feedback (not error correction), and vocabulary work, the students in Mr. Jacobs's class increased to an average of 4.69, or 1 point on the 7-point rubric. Is that a worthy impact? It's hard to judge because a 1-point average growth doesn't sound very impressive, so you need to calculate the effect size.

The next step in determining the effect size is to calculate standard deviation. Excel will do this as well[*]:

1. Type =STDEV and then select the student scores in the preassessment column again.

2. Do the same in the postassessment column.

3. Subtract the preassessment from the postassessment and then divide by the average of the two standard deviations.

Here's the formula:

$$\text{Effect size} = \frac{\text{Average (postassessment)} - \text{Average (Preassessment)}}{\text{Average standard deviation or SD}^{*}}$$

Teachers can calculate effect sizes for their classes and individual students to determine the impact their instruction and intervention have had.

[*]You can quickly calculate standard deviation on a number of websites, such as graphpad .com/quickcalcs/CImean1.cfm.

STUDENT WRITING DATA

Name	Pre	Post	Individual Effect Size
Alexander	3.5	4.5	1.15
Alexis	2.5	3	0.57
Alyssa	4	4.5	0.57
Ana	4	5.5	2.30
Andrea	3.5	5	1.72
Angel	4	6	2.30
Bianca	4	5	1.15
Caitlin	5	6	1.15
Elena	4	3.5	−0.57
Elisabeth	4	4.5	0.57
Emir	3.5	5	1.72
Gabriel	1.5	1.5	0.00
Giovanni	3	3.5	0.57
Irvin	3.5	5	1.72
Isaiah	5	5.5	0.57
Jerod	3.5	4	0.57
Jorge	3	4	1.15
Jose	4.5	5.5	1.15
Joshua	3.5	5	1.72
Kassandra	3.5	3	−0.57
Keneni	3.5	5	1.72
Komad	4	5	1.15
Makala	5	5.5	0.57
Marla	4.5	6	1.72
Michael	4	6	2.30
Nick	3	5	2.30
Santiago	3.5	4	0.57
Shakira	4.5	5.5	1.15
Veronica	4	5	1.15
Wendy	3	4	1.15
Yasmin	4	5	1.15
Average	**3.74**	**4.69**	
Standard Deviation	**0.74**	**1.03**	**0.88**
Effect Size	**1.08**		

Figure 5.1

In the writing example found in Figure 5.1, the standard deviation for the preassessment is 0.74, and the standard deviation for the postassessment is 1.03. The average of the two is 0.88. When the effect size is calculated using the formula above, it comes to 1.08, above our threshold of 0.40. Thus, Mr. Jacobs can conclude his efforts to improve his students' writing skills were successful. He can then infer that the focus on quality writing traits, receiving feedback, and vocabulary worked. As a note of caution, effect sizes do not establish causation. Mr. Jacobs cannot say with confidence that these specific actions caused the writing to be better, but he should be encouraged to share his approach with others so that they can determine the impact it might have on their students.

You may have noticed that the effect size is the average for the group. Mr. Jacobs really should say that the efforts to improve writing worked on average. That's why we suggest that teachers calculate effect sizes for individual students. It's pretty simple to do: subtract an individual student's preassessment score from his or her postassessment score and divide by the average standard deviation.

The formula looks like this:

$$\text{Effect size} = \frac{\text{Individual score (postassessment)} - \text{Individual score (preassessment)}}{\text{Average standard deviation or SD for the class}}$$

In this case, the majority of students are above the threshold of 0.40. Andrea, Emir, Irvin, Joshua, Keneni, and Marla really responded to the instruction they received. For these students, Mr. Jacobs should reflect on what was optimal about their learning.

As he noted, "These students seemed to really appreciate the feedback. They asked for more and more. They asked a lot of clarifying questions about their writing and submitted multiple drafts for every assignment, always looking to get better. The feedback seemed to really sink in with them."

Unfortunately, there was no effect on Gabriel.

As Mr. Jacobs noted, "Gabriel was out a lot, missing about 50% of the lessons. This is the last period of the day, and his mom picks him up a lot for medical appointments and therapy. I'm sure he needs it, but I think I should show her his achievement and see if we can work on a better schedule for him."

Elena and Kassandra experienced regression. Their scores declined, and the effect sizes were very low.

Mr. Jacobs, reflecting on his instruction, said, "I thought they'd do better. I thought that they were doing fine with the lessons. For some reason, this didn't work, and I owe it to them to schedule some additional instruction so that I can figure out what they need from me."

At the collective level, teachers can meet in grade-level groups or course-alike teams and engage in exactly the same process. For example, the fourth-grade team at Country Ranch Elementary School was focused on improving students' public speaking. The teachers collaborated on a series of lessons that included analyzing video of effective and ineffective public speakers, focusing on prosody (e.g., intonation, pauses, emphasis), and preparing and practicing speeches. At one of their grade-level meetings, they compared assessment results. Each teacher had submitted preassessment scores and averages, and standard deviations had been calculated. Six weeks later, the teachers collected benchmark data to make decisions about their impact. During their discussion, they noted that their effect size was only 0.30. As one of the teachers, Roxanne Campbell, commented, "The students don't seem to be getting much better at this."

In response, Alejandro Avila said, "Maybe they just need more time. They're only in fourth grade, so maybe we're expecting too much."

"I've been thinking about that," Ms. Campbell said. "But we want so much more for our students, Alejandro. Sharing thinking orally is an important skill, and we agreed that we should spend more time on it. Maybe it's not them; maybe it's us. Maybe we're not teaching this very well. I'm totally on board with teaching students public speaking, but I've never done it before, so I'm not sure what works."

"I've been thinking about this, too," Alyssa Rivera responded. "I don't think that my students understand that the speech should be like a paper. It has to have an introduction, a body, and a conclusion. I haven't had them write out their speeches because I didn't want them to read from the paper. I'm thinking that we might want to teach some concept mapping. That might help."

"I can see how that would also help with their writing," Mr. Avila added. "Maybe we're missing the writing and speaking connection. Okay, let's stay on this. I think we need some new lessons." At this point, the team of teachers got to work on new lessons that integrated writing and speaking. They focused on audience and teacher feedback as well.

When they met again six weeks later to discuss impact, the results were impressive. The average effect size had increased to 0.75, and all but three students had effect sizes that exceeded 0.40. The conversation was different, beginning with Mr. Avila, who said, "I know we're here to talk about the public speaking efforts, and the results are great. But I'd like to just make a quick note that the writing scores of my students have gone off the charts. They are really getting the expressive side of language. We are making a difference."

"Yes, and we're making an impact," Ms. Campbell added, "which will improve their lives in ways we can't even yet imagine."

Responding When There Is Insufficient Impact

Sometimes, despite our best efforts, students fail to respond to quality instruction. The only way to know if this has occurred is to regularly assess the impact we are having on students, as we discussed in the last chapter. When the impact is less than desirable, effective teachers try something different. They do not simply reteach the same lesson, perhaps slower or louder, hoping that students will get something out of it the second time around. Instead, they examine what worked and what didn't work, talk with colleagues, and redesign the learning opportunities for students.

For example, Haley Conrad analyzed her students' performance on a writing prompt and noted that several students failed to make progress. The students all knew what quality writing looked like. During the unit, Ms. Conrad and her students analyzed writing models to determine weak, average, good, and great papers. The students seemed to understand the expectations, but then did not meet them.

In their grade-level discussion, Ms. Conrad and her colleagues discussed ideas for reteaching the content. One idea that appealed to Ms. Conrad was to model her metacognitive strategies and write in front of her students, demonstrating the various decisions that she made as she drafted and edited her own work. She also focused her feedback on students' processing of the task, rather than simply focusing on their performance.

> EFFECT SIZE FOR
> METACOGNITIVE
> STRATEGIES = 0.69

> EFFECT SIZE FOR
> FEEDBACK = 0.75

The results were impressive, with significant gains made by students. As Ms. Conrad noted, "In the past, I would have graded the papers, and provided students with feedback—well, not really feedback, but more corrections—and then they would have fixed their papers and the class would have moved on. This time, I changed my approach because of students' needs. And they learned a lot more as a result."

Video 5.2
Evaluating Your Impact
Through Assessment

*http://resources.corwin.com/
VL-Literacy*

Teachers can engage in this type of response on a regular basis. Teaching is about making adjustments and trying to determine what will work for a particular group of students. As we have noted, there is no one right way to teach, and there are a lot of things that teachers do that are effective. Designing learning opportunities, monitoring for impact, and then making adjustments are the hallmark of effective teachers. But there are more formal ways to monitor impact.

Response to Intervention

The evidence for response to intervention (RTI) is significant; it's one of the top influences studied thus far with an effect size of 1.07. In other words, it works. There are several components of an effective RTI effort, which combine to produce the impact seen in the studies. These include universal screening, quality core instruction, progress monitoring, and

> EFFECT SIZE FOR
> RESPONSE TO
> INTERVENTION
> = 1.07

supplemental and intensive interventions. Entire books have been written on RTI (e.g., Fisher & Frey, 2010), so this section will only highlight the key components necessary for teachers to understand.

Screening

For RTI efforts to be most effective, school staff members have to screen students at the outset of the year. These screening tools are typically quick checks to identify students who may need additional intervention. In the realm of literacy, schools typically use some of the following: oral fluency measures, written responses, spelling inventories, or comprehension checks. A more comprehensive list of screening tools can be found at www.rti4success.org/resources/tools-charts/screening-tools-chart. Figure 5.2 contains an essential task list for progress monitoring to help guide you in your efforts.

For example, the teachers at Adams Middle School use *STAR Reading* (www.renaissance.com) to assess all of their students at the start of the year. This computer-adaptive assessment requires about 10 minutes per student, but it does cost to administer. At Adams, the first week of school focuses on building culture and climate with a wide range of activities to build trust between the faculty and students. As we noted in Chapter 1, positive teacher–student relationships have a strong impact. As part of the events during this time, students complete the reading assessment, learn about the technology policy, and get to know students across the grade span of the school. By the end of the week, the teachers at Adams have screening data on all of their students. They identify the students at risk of school failure and develop plans to accelerate their learning. This involves additional small group instruction for the targeted students during the school day as well as targeted vocabulary instruction provided by a reading specialist. As the weeks progress, the team monitors the progress of each of the students identified on the STAR tool, making sure that learning is progressing.

EFFECT SIZE FOR
TEACHER–STUDENT
RELATIONSHIPS
= 0.72

EFFECT SIZE FOR
ACCELERATION
= 0.68

The staff at Anza Springs Elementary School don't pay for their screening tool. They use a graded vocabulary inventory and a writing sample

ESSENTIAL TASK LIST FOR SCREENING TOOLS

Directions: In the second column, write the name(s) of the individual or team who will assume responsibility for the task identified in the first column. In the third column, write the deadline for or status of the task.

Task	Responsible Individual/ Team	Timeline/ Status
Review your screening instrument's items to be certain that content is aligned with the curriculum for each grade level.		
Once a tool has been selected, determine and secure the resources required to implement it.		
Determine initial professional development needs and continuing professional development support.		
Administer the screening measure three times a year (e.g., early fall, midterm, and late spring).		
Create a database that aligns with the screening instrument to hold student information and scores.		
Organize the screening results (e.g., graphs and tables) to provide a profile of all students and their comparisons with each other.		
Monitor results at the classroom level and make decisions about when teachers/instructional programs require more scrutiny and support.		
Add screening results to a database so that students' performance can be monitored over time.		
Specify written steps to follow when further scrutiny is needed for students judged to be at risk.		

Source: Johnson, Mellard, Fuchs, & McKnight (2006).

Figure 5.2

 Template available for download at **http://resources.corwin.com/VL-Literacy**

to identify students who may potentially need additional instruction and intervention. At Anza Springs, the teachers focus on direct instruction for the students who are at risk of not meeting expectations. As noted in Chapter 2, direct instruction requires that the teacher set clear learning targets and then provide students with practice on each target. The focus at Anza is on developing students' vocabulary knowledge because the teachers realize that their students, especially those living in poverty, have a significant gap in the conceptual and background knowledge that can be addressed with systematic vocabulary work.

EFFECT SIZE
FOR DIRECT
INSTRUCTION = 0.59

EFFECT SIZE
FOR VOCABULARY
PROGRAMS = 0.67

Quality Core Instruction

RTI efforts are based on the expectation that students receive quality core instruction as part of their ongoing participation in school. Also known as good first teaching, quality core instruction comprises Tier 1 of the RTI efforts. It's unreasonable to expect that all students receive supplemental and intensive interventions—there isn't time or money for that. If the vast majority of students are not being impacted by the regular classroom environment, we suggest that the tenets in this book may not be in place. In school systems that implement high-quality instruction, based on the influences on achievement outlined in this book, and then monitor the impact of those actions, fewer and fewer students need the extensive support offered through RTI. To our thinking, quality core instruction includes at least the following:

- Teacher clarity on, and communication about, the learning intentions and success criteria

- Student ownership of the expectations for learning

- Positive, humane, growth-producing teacher–student relationships

- Modeling and direct instruction of content

- Collaborative learning opportunities on a daily basis

- Small group learning based on instructional needs rather than perceived ability

- Spaced (rather than mass) independent practice and application of content

These are easy to write, and obvious to many, but not yet common in classrooms around the world. When these actions become the norm in classrooms, the need for additional interventions declines, and students learn more and better.

Progress Monitoring

Previous sections of this chapter focused on one aspect of progress monitoring—determining impact on learning. Teachers can ascertain whether or not the lessons they designed and delivered made a difference. And then, of course, they can take action. In RTI, teachers also monitor the progress, but they do so with two types of tools:

- **Curriculum-based measurements** (CBMs) are standardized assessments that have specific directions. These are usually timed and have specific scoring guidelines. CBMs are criterion-based tools that measure mastery of a skill. In essence, the tools help teachers determine if students have met the threshold, or criteria, established by the test maker. For example, the teachers at Bernardo Valley Elementary School use a published fluency measure to track student progress. They know that there is more to reading, and literacy, than fluency. And they know that fluency is a reasonable proxy for overall literacy development. When students are not making progress in their fluency development, the teachers look for clues about why and attempt to remedy the situation. Importantly, they do not simply drill students' oral reading speed, but rather they might examine students' decoding of multisyllabic words or check their sight reading skills or determine their vocabulary knowledge levels. When the teachers figure out what might be impeding a given student's fluency, they can address it and continue to monitor progress.

- **Curriculum-based assessments** (CBAs) are tools developed by teachers that align with the content they have taught. As Deno (1987) noted, CBAs involve "direct observation and recording of a student's performance in the local curriculum as a basis for gathering information to make instructional decisions" (p. 41). The teachers at Hancock Elementary School use their weekly

Direct instruction requires that the teacher set clear learning targets and then provide students with practice on each target.

spelling test as one of their CBAs. They collect and analyze data weekly, taking note of which students struggle with spelling, and intervene before it's too late. The Hancock teachers favor self-corrected spelling tests as an intervention, and nearly every student develops knowledge of words over the course of the year. The teachers at Harbor Middle School use course competencies as their CBA tool. The teachers for each course have identified key course expectations that students should master. The tools they use include essays, exams, projects, and performances. Students understand the expectations for each competency, including what success looks like on a given competency. Any student who does not pass the competency with at least 70% success is automatically provided supplemental instruction and intervention, which occur as push-in support in his or her classroom as well as tutorials during lunch and after school. The interventions are immediate and based on the content that a given student did not learn.

Notice that in each case, the progress monitoring tools that teachers use can result in students receiving supplemental or intensive interventions. Screening tools are important to identify students in need at the outset of the year, but progress monitoring tools ensure that students are noticed throughout the year. Figure 5.3 contains a series of reflection questions that school teams can ask themselves about their progress monitoring efforts.

Supplemental and Intensive Interventions

In each of the examples we have provided thus far in this chapter, the teachers organized additional interventions for students who demonstrated a need. Students were not left to figure it out on their own, nor did their teachers simply move on, accepting that some students failed to learn. RTI focuses efforts on providing evidence-based interventions for students who do not respond to quality core instruction (also known as Tier 1). In the language of RTI, students can receive Tier 2 or Tier 3 interventions, or a combination of both. This multitier system of support can result in improved student learning. It requires that teachers notice when students do not respond (when the impact is insufficient)

ESSENTIAL TASK LIST FOR PROGRESS MONITORING IN TIER 1

Directions: In the second column, write the name(s) of the individual or team who will assume responsibility for the task identified in the first column. In the third column, write the deadline for or status of the task.

Task	Responsible Individual/ Team	Timeline/ Status
Within the relevant content area, review the progress monitoring measure or tool selected for Tier 1 to determine whether content is aligned with your curriculum.		
Once a tool has been selected, determine and secure the resources required to implement it (e.g., computers, folders/copies, testing areas).		
Determine initial professional development needs and continuing professional development support.		
Implement a system of data collection and progress monitoring that includes determining both level and growth rate.		
Administer the progress monitoring measure frequently enough to assess a learner's responsiveness. At Tier 1, screening is three times a year, with routine monitoring weekly or twice weekly.		
Monitor results at the individual student level and make decisions about reasonable cut scores to determine movement to Tier 2 and beyond.		
Monitor results at the classroom level and make decisions about when teachers or instructional programs require more scrutiny and support.		

Source: Johnson, Mellard, Fuchs, & McKnight (2006).

Figure 5.3

 Template available for download at **http://resources.corwin.com/VL-Literacy**

and then change the instruction or intervention to reach the desired outcome. The two levels of response are

1. Tier 2, also known as supplemental interventions
2. Tier 3, also known as intensive interventions

In Jennifer Adams's fourth-grade class, four students have been identified on an initial screening tool as needing additional instruction or intervention in fluency. Ms. Adams does not simply drill these students' fluency, as she knows that doing so can accelerate their oral reading skills in the absence of the associated comprehension development. Instead, Ms. Adams meets with the students who need additional fluency work on a daily basis to provide small group, needs-based instruction. The rest of the class works collaboratively. When these students are not with Ms. Adams, they are working collaboratively with their peers, and other students are meeting with their teacher who focuses on other skills based on her assessments.

At the start of the year, Ms. Adams met with the four students and talked about the need for fluency development. As she said, "When you read fast enough, and hear it in your mind like someone talking, you understand more."

She had students write goals for their development. Yareli wanted to be like an actress, "with no stops to figure out the words," while Enrique identified the goal to "read as fast as Daniel."

As part of the discussions over the first few weeks of the year, Ms. Adams also talked about prosody—"sounding like a speaker," as she said to her students—and engaged in a series of lessons about pauses, intonation, emphasis, and the like. Over the next six weeks, two of the students made significant progress in fluency development. On their progress monitoring assessment, they scored within the 50th percentile for fourth grade, and Ms. Adams noted that they did not need to participate in Tier 2 interventions any longer.

As she noted, "The regular collaborative activities in our class will continue their fluency and comprehension development. When students engage in reader's theater, for example, they get a chance to practice fluency, comprehension, and having conversations. Also, as part of the buddy reading program our school uses, my students get to read aloud to students in first grade. They practice and practice their books, which also helps them develop fluency and prosody."

The two students who did not make sufficient progress were joined by a student new to the class who also did not score at expected levels on his fluency assessment. Ms. Adams changed the intervention to focus on rereading. As she said, "The metacognitive work on building fluency worked for a couple of students who needed it, but now I need to change it up so that the two who did not make enough progress have a different type of invention."

During the next six-week period, Ms. Adams worked with the three students who needed fluency development on reading and rereading texts so that they would experience fluent reading. They also talked about what they were reading between each successive read so that their comprehension was also maintained. She invited students to select the texts that they would read together to increase their motivation. Each of the three students nominated a text each week, and Ms. Adams reviewed the texts so that she would be ready with discussion questions. For example, Joshua wanted to read *What Do You Do With an Idea?* (Yamada, 2013). Ms. Adams developed some questions about the book to facilitate the students' comprehension, including these:

- What did the boy do when he first got his idea?
- When he told people about his idea, what happened?
- Why does the author capitalize "MY" when the boy decides to protect his idea?
- Let's review the artist's use of color. How does it change during the story?
- Do we ever learn what the boy's idea is?
- Do you have an idea that you are protecting?

The students read the text several times, talking about the questions raised by their teacher and their own perspectives on the story.

As Yareli said, "He says that he doesn't know where the idea came from. It musta popped into his head one day, but then he couldn't get rid of it."

As the students read, reread, and discussed the texts, Ms. Adams monitored their fluency. The students were seeing the power that reading fast enough, while sounding like a speaker, had on their understanding. At the end of the second six weeks, only one student performed below the 50% level.

Ms. Adams next decided to use the Neurological Impress Method (NIM) (Heckelman, 1969) with Joshua, the student who was still not making progress. The steps for NIM include the following:

- The teacher selects a text within the student's reading level.
- The teacher sits at the student's side so that he or she can speak into the student's ear.
- The student's finger rests on top of the teacher's finger as they read.
- The teacher moves his or her finger under each word as it is spoken.
- The teacher reads aloud slightly faster than the student reads aloud and models good fluency (chunking phrases and stopping where punctuation dictates).
- The teacher gives the "lead" to the student as the student becomes comfortable with the text.
- The student retells the text to the teacher at the completion of the NIM intervention and answers comprehension questions.

As Ms. Adams noted, "It's an older approach, but there is evidence that it works [e.g., Flood, Lapp, & Fisher, 2005], and I really need to figure something out so that Joshua makes progress. He is falling further and further behind, and my efforts with him have not yet had the level of impact I expect." At that point, Joshua moved to a Tier 3 intervention, receiving daily support from his teacher. In addition, a reading specialist met with Joshua. Based on a parent conversation, the best time for this additional intervention was first thing in the morning. Joshua's dad said that he could drop the boy off at least 30 minutes early so that he could meet with the specialist, Emily Cruz, before classes. Ms. Cruz decided to focus on multisyllabic word decoding because her assessment suggested that he also had difficulty with those words and slowed down when he encountered them.

Over the next six-week period, Joshua made progress, but had not yet reached the 50th percentile. Ms. Adams decided to continue her NIM, but Ms. Cruz changed her intervention to focus on public speaking. As she said, "I am wondering about Josh's confidence and his level of understanding about what speech should sound like. I think it might help if he saw a reason for building his fluency. He told me that he'd like to perform, maybe in band or in the school play, so I made the connection for him that practicing and public speaking were important. We read, and reread, texts together, and then he performs them for me. We've developed an amazing relationship, and we laugh every day."

By the end of the school year, Joshua (who had arrived later in the school year) had made significant progress. His fluency scores were in the 70% percentile, and his comprehension was nearly grade level. In addition, his confidence soared. Joshua was clearly proud of his accomplishments, and his parents noted, "He worked really hard for this, and we ask him all the time how it feels to be making so much progress. He says that it's easy because there are people who like him, and they let him read interesting things."

The impact that Ms. Adams and Ms. Cruz had on Joshua, and countless other students, was significant. Their ability to rally resources around students in need, while not neglecting the education of others, is a model for visible literacy learning. They didn't accept low levels of learning; they implemented actions they believed would result in learning, and they monitored and adjusted to obtain the impact they expected.

Of course, RTI can be implemented on a much wider scale than occurred in Ms. Adams's class. Figure 5.4 includes a list of tasks that should be noted as teachers and school teams monitor students' progress in Tiers 2 and 3. In some schools, this is done collaboratively, at the grade or department level. We'll consider two examples of this. Note the collective teacher efficacy involved as groups of teachers examine the impact they have had and then design interventions to ensure that all students learn.

ESSENTIAL TASK LIST FOR PROGRESS MONITORING IN TIERS 2 AND 3

Directions: In the second column, write the name(s) of the individual or team who will assume responsibility for the task identified in the first column. In the third column, write the deadline for or status of the task.

Task	Responsible Individual/ Team	Timeline/ Status
Implement a system of data collection and progress monitoring that includes determining both level and growth rate.		
Within the relevant area of focus for the intervention, review the progress monitoring measure or tool selected for Tier 2 and beyond to determine whether content is aligned with the intervention.		
Administer the progress monitoring measure frequently enough to assess a learner's responsiveness. At Tier 2, two to five times per week is the research-based recommendation.		
Organize results to provide a profile of the student's progress within this tier. This could be a graph of test scores supplemented with student work samples.		
Monitor results to determine whether a student is responding to the intervention.		
Develop decision rules about when to return a student to Tier 1, when to continue with Tier 2 and beyond, and whether further scrutiny of student performance for special education is warranted.		

Source: Johnson, Mellard, Fuchs, & McKnight (2006).

Figure 5.4

 Template available for download at **http://resources.corwin.com/VL-Literacy**

The kindergarten teachers at Casa del Sol Elementary have high expectations for their students, most of whom live in poverty and many of whom speak a language in addition to English. For example, they expect their students to know the names of all letters (upper- and lowercase) by November 1. They expect students to know 100 sight words by the end of the school year (from a list of 150). They also expect that all of their students move from emergent spelling, in which writers use scribbles, letters, and letter-like forms together but don't associate the marks they make with any specific phonemes, to letter-name or alphabetic spelling, in which writers represent phonemes in words with letters. As a side note, over 50% of the kindergarten students at Casa del Sol move into the third level of spelling development, within-word pattern spelling, in which writers can spell most one-syllable short-vowel words and learn to spell long-vowel patterns and *r*-controlled vowels.

At the start of the year, each kindergarten teacher engages his or her class in a series of activities that include screening tools. These activities are designed to be engaging and low stress. The teachers integrate simple assessments into the tasks. For example, the teachers tell a story about a cat that gets lost and has to be rescued. Students are invited to write about how they could help find the cat. Over the first week, each student is also individually assessed on his or her letter and sight word knowledge.

At their first team meeting, the teachers examine the data and discuss the needs for the current cohort of students. When discussing the letter knowledge, Frank Gibson noted, "Over half of our students this year already know all of the capital letters. I think we're going to need to make some changes to our instruction and accelerate that part." The other teachers agreed.

Elvida Vasquez added, "But we have 16 students who scored zero, not knowing any of their letters. We can't leave them behind. But I agree that we don't want to hold others back while we focus on the 16."

During the course of their meeting, the teachers developed a plan to implement a number of Tier 2 and 3 interventions. The plan involved developing a listening station that could be used by students who had more advanced knowledge of reading. At that station, students used earbuds to listen to a teacher reading to them while also talking about the text through a think-aloud. The teachers decided to take turns recording their voice so that students would hear different adults talking.

One of the lessons involved the text *Goodnight Moon* (Brown, 1947). The listening started out with the reader saying, "Is your book in front of you? Do you see the title, *Goodnight Moon*? Put your finger on the title. Check your partner. Is everyone ready?" The reading continued with the teacher reading pages, pausing to think aloud. For example, when they got to the page that says "and two little kittens and a pair of mittens" (n.p.), the teacher said, "Let me see if I can find them. Oh, there, on the side, I see the mittens. They are hanging up by the boots. I see the fireplace there, so I'm thinking that the mittens must have gotten wet. I bet it was cold outside if they needed their mittens and boots. I also see the kittens. It looks like one of them is going to jump. See that? Let's talk about what else we see on this page. Please set the time for two minutes and take turns talking. Put the recording on pause and come back when the timer rings."

Engaging students in the listening station provided teachers with time to focus on other students' needs. The teachers worked with some students on sight words and other students on letter recognition. They collected data about their students' progress on a regular basis, looking for trends. By November 1, all but six students could name all of the upper- and lowercase letters. At that point, just over 40% of the students had moved into letter-name or alphabetic spelling, and a handful of students were beyond that. The team met to talk about the six students who had not yet mastered letter names and decided to provide Tier 3 individual interventions for them. The teachers also asked their resource specialist to spend time with these students, also focusing on letter names and sounds. They set up weekly tracking data and agreed to report to each other about the progress these six students made each week.

The team also noted that there was a small group of students in each class who had not made much progress on their sight words. The teachers agreed to focus Tier 2 efforts on these students, scheduling additional small group instruction several times per week with each group.

As Lupita Camacho said, "I think it's worth it to focus additional efforts and support on these students now so that we don't end up with a crisis later. I mean, they're making progress but not as much as they could."

"I think we need to change our after-school practice assignments," Staci Clarke. "Most of these students attend our after-school program. Maybe they could play games with sight words, like Concentration and Bingo. That could help. At least it wouldn't hurt, and it might reinforce the knowledge of the students who already know the words."

The team agreed and asked Ms. Clarke to talk with the after-school program staff.

Over the course of the year, these kindergarten teachers tracked student progress and continued to make adjustments so that they could obtain the results they expected. Students moved in and out of Tier 2 and 3 interventions, based on the data. The teachers discussed student progress at their biweekly meetings and adjusted the learning environment accordingly.

The same thing was done with the ninth-grade English team at Amelia Earhart High School. They focused on writing because, as they often said, every writer can read, but not every reader can write. This team focused on different aspects of writing every three weeks and monitored students' progress collaboratively. Consistent with RTI, they screened all of their students at the start of the year, noting which students were significantly delayed in their writing development.

As Michael Mendoza noted, "We have about eight students in each class who are pretty far behind. That's too many for Tier 3, so we should prioritize. I would say that students learning English, who already have a language support class, could be in Tier 2 for us and those who do not could be in Tier 3."

The other teachers in the department agreed. Each identified students on his or her roster who met the criteria for supplemental interventions, and the team worked on ideas for writing improvement.

"Based on our review of their writing," said Katelyn Castillo, "I think the starting place with this group is introductions. If we can get the students to develop strong intros, maybe their ideas will flow a bit better in the rest of their work." The team quickly agreed, and Julianna Dodd offered to develop some sample lessons that the team could use. She found a resource that included 12 types of introductions (see Figure 5.5) and developed a series of lessons to improve students' writing that she shared with her team. As part of the lessons, students learned to analyze the writing of others (including professional writers) to notice how they engaged readers. For example, Ms. Dodd used the introduction to *Jack Plank Tells Tales* by Natalie Babbitt (2007) to highlight the ways that authors use description:

> Jack Plank was an out of work pirate. He'd had a job, and a good job, too, on a lovely ship called the *Avarice*. But the thing is, Jack wasn't good at plundering. There's only one way to plunder: You have to yell and make faces and rattle your sword, and once you've got people scared, you take things away from them. That's what pirates do. But Jack didn't seem to have a knack for it.

As students' writing of introductions progressed, the team met to talk about next steps. The teachers agreed to give all of their students a compare-and-contrast writing task as a progress monitoring tool. Each teacher reviewed his or her students' writing and put a student's initials next to an error, such as lacking information from two sources. As a group, the ninth-grade teachers analyzed the patterns of error to determine what to do next. A sample analysis of one teacher's class is included in Figure 5.6 on page 160. Notice that this analysis lends itself to making decisions about reteaching. In some cases, individual students need additional instruction, as was the case with two students (one in Period 1 and another in Period 4). Given the focus on writing introductions earlier in the year, the teachers were pleased to see that very few students still needed work in this area. Those who did would receive intensive interventions.

In other cases, there are small groups of students who need additional instruction and/or intervention. For example, there is a small group of students in each period who need more work on mechanics. There are also small groups of students who need to include information from sources and others who need to focus on including evidence. Simply editing students' writing and then returning their papers to them would not have resulted in the focused conversations these ninth-grade teachers had

TYPES OF INTRODUCTIONS

Action	events happening from the onset
Anecdote	an amusing or biographical tale
Description	a "showing, not telling" description of a place, event, or character
Detail	an attentive, focused look at something in particular
Dialogue	a significant conversation between or among characters
Emotion	a profound feeling
Interesting fact	some noteworthy evidence
Setting	the time and place where action occurs
Startling statement	a shocking, astounding, extraordinary, or unusual statement
Thoughts	deep thoughts; worthy of note
Question	a query that elicits thinking about your topic or theme
Quotation	a passage, excerpt, or selection from a recognized source or person

Source: Medina (2006).

Figure 5.5

about what to do next to impact their students' writing development. Interestingly, a significant number of students in Period 1 needed additional instruction on transitions. This issue was not generalized to the other classes this teacher taught.

Reflecting on this, the teacher commented, "If I didn't have this error analysis data, and time to talk with my colleagues about responding when we don't have the impact we desire, I would probably have taught all of my classes about transitions. I would have wasted so much time for the majority of my students. This allows me to be much more precise. I don't have time to waste, and focusing on the patterns of error allows all of us to pinpoint needs and make adjustments."

Supplemental and intensive interventions have the potential to positively impact students' learning when they are based on accurate assessment data

Topic: Compare-and-Contrast Essay

Error	Period 1	Period 2	Period 3	Period 4	Period 5
Introductory paragraph contains summary of similarities and differences that will be addressed	JR	PREP		AT	
Comparison paragraph(s) includes information from both texts	JR, JT, AG, DL, TV	PREP	EC, MV, WK	AT, SK, MG, EM, BA, TS	HH, DP, MR, CH
Comparison paragraph(s) includes evidence from both texts	JR, DD, AG, SL	PREP	WK, MW	AT, BA	MR
Contrast paragraph(s) includes information from both texts	JR, JT, DL, MM, SL, ST, ND	PREP	RT, VE, VD, CC	AT, MG, SC, PM, LG	DP, DE
Contrast paragraph(s) includes evidence from both texts	JR, DS	PREP	SJ, JM	AT, TR, PC	DE
Transitions between paragraphs lead the reader logically	AA, TA, AC, TC, JC, UC, DD, RD, TE, RE, FE, MF, AG, JJ, SL, JR, JT, DL, AM, PM, MM, JM, HN, AO, CS, TS, ST, TT, ND, AZ, DZ	PREP	WK, RT, AG, SJ	AT, MG, BA, GL, DO, DE, LR	SR, DC, MF
Mechanics interfere with reading	JR, JT, MM, AZ, DZ	PREP	EC, AG, SJ	AT, DW, DL, KS, IP, SN, MW, JG, KE, JV	DE, MR, DC, AT

Source: Frey & Fisher (2013a). Copyright © 2013 by the National Council of Teachers of English. Reprinted with permission.

Figure 5.6

and when students have instruction that addresses their needs. In general, Tier 2 interventions involve the teacher meeting with small groups of students while the rest of the class completes other tasks. Importantly, we hope that the implementation of RTI does not mean that the rest of the class is assigned boring busywork (or shut-up sheets). Instead, we hope students are engaged in collaborative and productive tasks, especially the kind that deepen their knowledge, while the teachers meet with small groups to address need. In some cases, small group instruction does not allow for breakthrough results, and more intensive interventions are needed. Often, these interventions are provided by experts outside of the classroom, but classroom teachers can be involved in intensive interventions as well. The logistics of RTI can be complex, but the key message in this approach is that all students can learn if we are willing to examine our impact and adjust the learning environment accordingly.

> What most students who struggle need is not more of the same, but demonstrably different and better instruction.

Learning From What Doesn't Work

Thus far, we have focused our attention on influences that can positively impact students' learning. We explored surface, deep, and transfer levels of learning and noted that there are some things that work better at each level. We also discussed the ways in which teachers can determine their impact on student learning, and then respond when the impact is not as expected. Now, it's time to focus on some things that really don't work to build students' literacy lives. We don't want teachers to undo all of their hard work by engaging in practices that are harmful or that waste valuable learning time. Unfortunately, these are all too common in use. Even worse, many of these practices are the result of not focusing on one's impact, and instead spending time cataloging a student's shortcomings.

Grade-Level Retention

Students are often retained in a grade level based on their literacy achievement. The meta-analyses of this indicate that the practice is actually having the reverse effect, with an effect size of –0.13. As Frey (2005) and others have noted, grade-level retention for literacy achievement is not a defensible practice. But schools and districts still hold onto the hope that another year of schooling will ensure that students learn to read and write at higher levels. Why would another year of the same curriculum, often using the same type of teaching and the same assessment tasks, make a difference? What most students who struggle

> EFFECT SIZE FOR RETENTION = –0.13

need is not more of the same, but demonstrably different and better instruction, and teachers would be wise to consider RTI (e.g., Fisher & Frey, 2010), which has an effect size of 1.07. In most RTI efforts, students receive supplemental and intensive interventions throughout the year, delivered by knowledgeable adults who can monitor and adjust as needed to reach a desired level of achievement.

Ability Grouping

Another lesson educators should learn focuses on ability grouping. Simply said, there is no evidence to suggest that this practice will yield breakthrough results. The effect size of ability grouping is 0.12, negligible in terms of impact yet common in many schools. Some people argue that ability grouping works for advanced students, even if it doesn't work for struggling learners. The problem is, it's not true. The effect of ability grouping is to disrupt the learning community, socially ostracize some learners, and compromise social skills, to name a few (Sapon-Shevin, 1994). And the effect on minority groups is much more serious, with more minority students likely to be in lower-ability classes destined to demonstrate to low performance often with the least effective teachers (Jimerson, 2001).

We have lost count of the number of times we have talked with well-meaning educators who hope that the solution to their students' literacy achievement lies in grouping students by their perceived ability. Taking a grade level of students and giving one teacher the lowest-performing students, another teacher the average-performing students, and yet another the highest-performing students may be popular, but the evidence is clear that it is not the answer. The two most common forms of ability grouping are

- **Within-class grouping**—putting students into groups based on the results of an assessment

- **Between-class grouping**—separating students into different classes, courses, or course sequences (curricular tracks) based on their previous academic achievement

The risk in writing this is that some readers will overgeneralize. Within-class and between-class ability grouping should be avoided. But *needs-based* instruction, with flexible groups, should not be eliminated. Student-centered teaching, basing instructional actions on students' understanding and then engaging students in small group learning, can be very effective. In fact, small group learning has an effect size of 0.49—provided the grouping is flexible, not fixed. The key to this approach is the condition that the groups change, and the instruction must match the needs of the learner. Let's look at the difference, occurring at the same school. In one sixth-grade classroom, the teacher administered a writing assessment and grouped her students based on their scores. The students with the lowest scores were in one group, slightly better writers formed a second group, and so on. She then met with groups over several weeks, providing instruction to each group. Sounds familiar and logical, right? It just didn't work. The postassessments were no different from the original samples. The lowest-performing writers were still the lowest, but their scores inched up a barely perceptible amount. That was a lot of work for very little benefit.

> EFFECT SIZE FOR
> SMALL GROUP
> LEARNING = **0.49**

Down the hall, another sixth-grade teacher administered the same writing assessment. She then analyzed the patterns of error found in her students' writing and continually regrouped students daily based on the error patterning. On one day, she met with a group of students who needed guidance with transitions and then with another group of students who needed support with maintaining voice. On another day, she focused her small group instruction on students who changed point of view in their writing and on another group of students with erroneous spelling patterns. In the same amount of time as was available to her colleague, she was able to address many of the instructional needs of her students using small groups. And the results speak for themselves. The average score increased a full performance level, and there wasn't a single student left in the lowest band on the rubric.

> Student-centered teaching can be very effective. In fact, small group learning has an effect size of 0.49—provided the grouping is flexible, not fixed.

As this teacher said, "I know my impact because I calculate it myself. I want to know if what I'm doing works." These may seem like subtle differences, but they are important. Small group instruction is effective, but not when the intervention for the students is the ability of the group. The groups have to be flexible so that the instruction each group receives aligns with the students' performance and understanding.

Video 5.3
Assessment:
Needs-Based Grouping

*http://resources.corwin.com/
VL-Literacy*

Matching Learning Styles With Instruction

Another practice that has become widespread, but for which there is no supporting evidence, is matching learning styles with instruction. It may very well be that there are differences in how we prefer to access and share information, and that preference may change in different situations with different groups of people, but teaching students based on our perception of their particular type of intelligence is of very limited value. In fact, the effect size is 0.17. We know a student—we'll call him Musab. He loves music. He has earbuds in anytime they're allowed. He quotes rap songs in response to questions and essay prompts. He sings quietly in the halls and performs in every talent show the school offers. He can listen to a tune and immediately replicate it on a piano. Some might say that he is gifted in the area of music. Others might say that his preferred learning style is musical. Does that mean he is excused from developing interpersonal skills? Should we excuse his errors in writing? Should his teachers be encouraged to sing their lessons and rap their instructions? And if he's in class with students who have other preferences, should we separate him? *No.* Matching instruction with a perception of a learning style is not going to radically raise reading and writing achievement. Why condemn Musab to one form of learning (via music), when indeed he may need to be taught other ways to learn? Let's acknowledge that there are differences in learners, but let's not label students (and not labeling students is really effective, with an effect size of 0.61). Instead, let's focus on instructional routines and habits that will ensure all students learn at high levels. Teachers may need to use multiple methods to capitalize on multiple ways of learning, but the mistake is to categorize students into one or more learning styles.

> EFFECT SIZE
> FOR MATCHING
> LEARNING
> STYLES = 0.17

> EFFECT SIZE FOR
> NOT LABELING
> STUDENTS = 0.61

Test Prep

Test prep, including teaching test-taking skills, is another area for which there is insufficient evidence to warrant continued use. We've all done it because there is an appeal to one's surface logic to teaching students generic test-taking skills. It just wastes a lot of precious time. Instead, teach learning and test-taking skills as an integral part of every lesson (not as a separate subject)—focus on teaching students the content and how to learn this content—as this has been shown to be much more effective in increasing student achievement on external measures of success. That's not to say that students shouldn't understand the format of the test, but that only takes a short time. They should also be taught about how to best prioritize time doing any task, as this can be a critical test-prep skill—but again do this within the context of the regular lessons—not some stand-alone skill. Test prep and teaching test-taking skills are consuming significant numbers of instructional minutes, despite the fact that we know there is no evidence that these accountability measures are going to inherently improve instruction or learning (Hattie, 2014). We are currently stuck with these types of tests, and students will likely face a wide range of tests over their lives (college admissions, food handling, and driving, to name a few). Studying content, and how to learn this content, especially using effective study skills techniques will pay much better dividends than trying to figure out how to beat the test.

> EFFECT SIZE FOR TEACHING TEST-TAKING AND COACHING = **0.27**

> EFFECT SIZE FOR STUDY SKILLS = **0.63**

Homework

The final lesson we offer with respect to learning from what doesn't work, despite the fact that there are others, focuses on homework. Overall, homework has little impact on students' learning, with an effect size of 0.29. In this case, it's worth it to examine the value of homework at different grade levels. At the elementary level, homework has a limited impact on student learning, with an effect size of 0.10. At the middle school level, the effect size is 0.30, whereas at the high school level, the effect size is 0.55. The major reason for these differences comes from the nature of homework. Homework that provides another chance to practice something already taught and for which a student has the beginnings of mastery can be effective (and much high school homework is of this nature), but homework that involves new materials, projects, or work with which a student may struggle when alone is least effective (and too much elementary homework is of this nature). Importantly, homework may not be the answer to students' achievement, and efforts

> EFFECT SIZE FOR HOMEWORK = **0.29**

> EFFECT SIZE FOR ELEMENTARY SCHOOL HOMEWORK = **0.10**

> EFFECT SIZE FOR HIGH SCHOOL HOMEWORK = **0.55**

to raise the rigor of schooling by assigning more independent learning that students complete at home are misguided and potentially harmful. Students can succeed just as much from what they do in school. Do not ask them to create a school at home where many students need adult expertise; while nearly all parents want to help their students, some do not know how. Many parents can be poor teachers of schoolwork!

Thus far, we have focused on actions that do not work. We could have also focused on the finger-pointing common in some schools. Yes, mobility has a negative impact on students' learning, as does summer vacation. Hattie (2012) noted that about 50% of the achievement variation found in schools is attributed to student characteristics and demographics. Unfortunately, in many schools, that 50% gets all the play. After the students themselves, teachers have the biggest impact on student achievement, followed by school effects, the principal, parents, and the home. This is really, really important: a significant amount of the variance in student achievement is attributed to teachers. What teachers do matters. How teachers think really matters. Making informed decisions about what actions to take, based on evidence, should be the focus of professional development sessions and grade-level or department conversations rather than admiring problems and blaming students for the conditions in which they live.

> Efforts to raise the rigor of schooling by assigning more homework are misguided and potentially harmful.

Conclusion

Measuring one's impact on student learning means that assessment is a prominent feature of the classroom. The purpose is not to grade the students' work, but to measure progress and compare it to the teaching that has occurred. Daily formative assessment is a chief way for teachers to make instructional decisions about what will occur next. Ways to check for understanding include asking questions, using exit tickets, and giving students lots of opportunities to self-assess. But these remain moment-in-time snapshots if not further contextualized through the administration and analysis of pre- and postassessments and regularly paced progress monitoring. The assessments discussed in this chapter are a reminder of the many ways we have of tracking student progress. But it's what we do with them that counts. If assessment is used for nothing more than sorting students, we will continue to achieve the results we have always gotten. These assessments are measures of *our* progress, too—but only if we choose to look closely at our impact.

The risk to our students in failing to examine our impact is significant and damaging. The reliance on ineffective practices, such as in-grade retention and ability grouping, is the result of decisions by well-meaning but misguided adults who have focused their attention on the characteristics of students at the exclusion of the effectiveness of the instruction they have received. We should know our students well, and teach to their strengths while closely monitoring learning gaps. But the evidence is clear. Although what the student brings to school in terms of his or her learning background is important, a significant percentage of achievement variance lies within the teacher's influence (Hattie, 2009). Yet too often the vigor with which teachers locate explanations that lie with the student far outstrips their efforts to examine their impact on student learning and adjust accordingly.

This book has been about empowering educators to do exactly that. The profession is filled with dedicated people who have devoted their professional careers to improving the literacy lives of children. Literacy matters. And the good news is that teachers matter. We mean this not as coffee-cup sentimentality, but rather as an empowering sentiment. What teachers do matters when they scale learning to move from surface, to deep, to transfer of learning, and match approaches to their students' conceptual levels of knowledge. What teachers do matters when they monitor their impact and use that information to inform instruction and intervention. What teachers do matters when they reject institutional practices that harm learning. And best of all, what teachers do matters when they make literacy learning visible to their students, so students can become their own teachers.

> After the students themselves, teachers have the biggest impact on student achievement.

Video 5.4
Visible Learning:
Three Keys

*http://resources.corwin.com/
VL-Literacy*

Rank	Influence	ES
1	Self-reported grades/student expectations	1.44
2	Piagetian programs	1.28
*3	Response to intervention	1.07
*4	Teacher credibility	0.90
5	Providing formative evaluation	0.90
6	Micro-teaching	0.88
*7	Classroom discussion	0.82
8	Comprehensive interventions for students who are learning disabled	0.77
9	Teacher clarity	0.75
10	Feedback	0.75
11	Reciprocal teaching	0.74
12	Teacher–student relationships	0.72
13	Spaced versus mass practice	0.71
14	Metacognitive strategies	0.69
15	Acceleration	0.68
16	Classroom behavioral	0.68
17	Vocabulary programs	0.67
18	Repeated reading programs	0.67
19	Creativity programs on achievement	0.65
20	Prior achievement	0.65
21	Self-verbalization and self-questioning	0.64
22	Study skills	0.63
23	Teaching strategies	0.62
24	Problem-solving teaching	0.61
25	Not labeling students	0.61
26	Comprehension programs	0.60
27	Concept mapping	0.60
28	Cooperative versus individualistic learning	0.59
29	Direct instruction	0.59
30	Tactile stimulation programs	0.58
31	Mastery learning	0.58
32	Worked examples	0.57
33	Visual perception programs	0.55

(Continued)

Rank	Influence	ES
34	Peer tutoring	0.55
35	Cooperative versus competitive learning	0.54
36	Phonics instruction	0.54
*37	Student-centered teaching	0.54
38	Classroom cohesion	0.53
39	Pre-term birth weight	0.53
40	Keller's Master Learning	0.53
41	Peer influences	0.53
42	Classroom management	0.52
43	Outdoor/adventure programs	0.52
44	Home environment	0.52
45	Socio-economic status	0.52
46	Interactive video methods	0.52
47	Professional development	0.51
48	Goals	0.50
49	Play programs	0.50
50	Second/third chance programs	0.50
51	Parental involvement	0.49
52	Small group learning	0.49
53	Questioning	0.48
54	Concentration/persistence/engagement	0.48
55	School effects	0.48
56	Motivation	0.48
57	Quality of teaching	0.48
58	Early interventions	0.47
59	Self-concept	0.47
60	Preschool programs	0.45
61	Writing programs	0.44
62	Expectations	0.43
63	School size	0.43
64	Science	0.42
65	Cooperative learning	0.42
66	Exposure to reading	0.42
67	Behavioral organizers/adjunct questions	0.41

Rank	Influence	ES
68	Mathematics programs	0.40
69	Reducing anxiety	0.40
70	Social skills programs	0.39
71	Integrated curricula programs	0.39
72	Enrichment	0.39
73	Principals/school leaders	0.39
74	Career interventions	0.38
75	Time on task	0.38
*76	Psychotherapy programs	0.38
77	Computer-assisted instruction	0.37
78	Adjunct aids	0.37
79	Bilingual programs	0.37
80	Drama/arts programs	0.35
81	Creativity related to achievement	0.35
82	Attitude to mathematics/science	0.35
83	Frequent/effects of testing	0.34
84	Decreasing disruptive behavior	0.34
*85	Various teaching on creativity	0.34
86	Simulations	0.33
87	Inductive teaching	0.33
88	Ethnicity	0.32
89	Teacher effects	0.32
90	Drugs	0.32
91	Inquiry-based teaching	0.31
*92	Systems accountability	0.31
93	Ability grouping for gifted students	0.30
94	Homework	0.29
95	Home visiting	0.29
96	Exercise/relaxation	0.28
97	Desegregation	0.28
98	Teaching test-taking and coaching	0.27
99	Use of calculators	0.27

(Continued)

Rank	Influence	ES
*100	Volunteer tutors	0.26
101	Lack of illness	0.25
102	Mainstreaming	0.24
103	Values/moral education programs	0.24
104	Competitive versus individualistic learning	0.24
105	Programmed instruction	0.23
106	Summer school	0.23
107	Finances	0.23
108	Religious schools	0.23
109	Individualized instruction	0.22
110	Visual/audio-visual methods	0.22
111	Comprehensive teaching reforms	0.22
*112	Teacher verbal ability	0.22
113	Class size	0.21
114	Charter schools	0.20
115	Aptitude/treatment interactions	0.19
116	Extra-curricular programs	0.19
117	Learning hierarchies	0.19
118	Co-/team teaching	0.19
119	Personality	0.18
120	Within-class grouping	0.18
121	Special college programs	0.18
122	Family structure	0.18
*123	School counseling effects	0.18
124	Web-based learning	0.18
125	Matching learning styles	0.17
126	Teacher immediacy	0.16
127	Home-school programs	0.16
128	Problem-based learning	0.15
129	Sentence-combining programs	0.15
130	Mentoring	0.15
131	Ability grouping	0.12

Rank	Influence	ES
132	Diet	0.12
133	Gender	0.12
134	Teacher education	0.12
135	Distance education	0.11
136	Teacher subject matter knowledge	0.09
*137	Changing school calendar/timetable	0.09
138	Out-of-school curricular experiences	0.09
139	Perceptual motor programs	0.08
140	Whole language	0.06
*141	Diversity of students	0.05
142	College halls of residence	0.05
143	Multi-grade/age classes	0.04
144	Student control over learning	0.04
145	Open versus traditional learning spaces	0.01
146	Summer vacation	−0.02
147	Welfare policies	−0.12
148	Retention	−0.13
149	Television	−0.18
150	Mobility	−0.34

Source: Hattie (2012). Reproduced with permission.

* Represents an effect that has been added to the original list since the publication of *Visible Learning: A Synthesis of Over 800 Meta-Analyses Relating to Achievement* (Hattie, 2009).

Note: Effect size for collective teacher efficacy published separately in Hattie (2015), The Applicability of Visible Learning to Higher Education, *Scholarship of Teaching and Learning in Psychology, 1*(1), 79–91. In-chapter references to effect sizes for mnemonics, taking class notes, organizing and transforming conceptual knowledge, and teaching students to summarize are not listed here and are based on the ongoing synthesis of learning strategies research.

References

Adams, G. L., & Engelmann, S. (1996). *Research on direct instruction: 20 years beyond DISTAR*. Seattle, WA: Educational Achievement Systems.

Almasi, J. F. (1994). The nature of fourth graders' sociocognitive conflicts in peer-led and teacher-led discussions of literature. *Reading Research Quarterly, 3*(3), 314–351.

Anderson, R. C., Wilson, P. T., & Fielding, L. G. (1988). Growth in reading and how children spend their time outside school. *Reading Research Quarterly, 23,* 285–303.

Applegate, K. (2011). *The one and only Ivan.* New York, NY: HarperCollins.

Babbitt, N. (2007). *Jack Plank tells tales.* New York, NY: Scholastic.

Bahekar, A. A., Singh, S., Saha, S., Molnar, J., & Arora, R. (2007). The prevalence and incidence of coronary heart disease is significantly increased in periodontitis: A meta-analysis. *American Heart Journal, 154*(5), 830–837.

Baker, S., Simmons, D., & Kame'enui, E. (1998). *Vocabulary acquisition: Synthesis of the research.* Washington, DC: U.S. Department of Education, Office of Educational Research and Improvement, Educational Resources Information Center.

Bear, D. R., Invernizzi, M., Templeton, S., & Johnston, F. (2011). *Words their way: Word study for phonics, vocabulary, and spelling instruction* (5th ed.). Upper Saddle River, NJ: Pearson.

Beck, I. L., McKeown, M. G., & Kucan, L. (2013). *Bringing words to life: Robust vocabulary instruction* (2nd ed.). New York, NY: Guilford Press.

Bereiter, C. (2002). *Education and mind in the knowledge age.* Hillsdale, NJ: Erlbaum.

Bereiter, C., & Scardamalia, M. (1982). From conversation to composition: The role of instruction in a developmental process. In R. Glaser (Ed.), *Advances in instructional psychology* (Vol. 2, pp. 1–64). Hillsdale, NJ: Erlbaum.

Berkeley, S., Marshak, L., Mastropieri, M. A., & Scruggs, T. E. (2011). Improving student comprehension of social studies text: A self-questioning strategy for inclusive middle school classes. *Remedial & Special Education, 32*(2), 105–113.

Biemiller, A. (2005). Size and sequence in vocabulary development: Implications for choosing words for primary grade vocabulary instruction. In E. H. Hiebert & M. L. Kamil (Eds.), *Teaching and learning vocabulary: Bringing research to practice* (pp. 223–242). Mahwah, NJ: Erlbaum.

Biggs, J. (1999). *Teaching for quality learning at university.* Buckingham, UK: Society for Research Into Higher Education and Open University Press.

Bintz, W. P., & Williams, L. (2005). Questioning techniques of fifth and sixth grade reading teachers. *Middle School Journal, 37*(1), 45–52.

Bogard, J., & McMackin, M. (2012). Combining traditional and new literacies in a 21st-century writing workshop. *Reading Teacher, 65*(5), 313–323.

Bradbury, R. (1953). *Fahrenheit 451.* New York, NY: Ballantine Books.

Bransford, J. D., Brown, A. L., & Cocking, R. R. (Eds.). (2000). *How people learn: Brain, mind, experience, and school.* Committee on Developments in the Science of Learning and Committee on Learning Research and Educational Practice. Washington, DC: National Academy Press.

Brookhart, S. M. (2008). *How to give effective feedback to your students.* Alexandria, VA: ASCD.

Brown, M. W. (1947). *Goodnight moon.* New York, NY: Harper & Row.

Burek, D., & Losos, C. (2014). Debate: Where speaking and listening come first. *Voices From the Middle, 22*(1), 49–57.

Campbell, J. (1949). *The hero with a thousand faces.* New York, NY: Pantheon Books.

Cazden, C. B. (1988). *Classroom discourse: The language of teaching and learning.* Portsmouth, NH: Heinemann.

Chesky, J., & Hiebert, E. H. (1987). The effects of prior knowledge and audience on high school students' writing. *Journal of Educational Research, 80,* 304–313.

Chesterton, G. K. (2004, March 7). The fallacy of success. In *All things considered.* The Project Gutenberg. Retrieved from http://www.gutenberg.org/files/11505/11505-h/11505-h.htm (Original work published 1915)

Clay, M. M. (1979). *Preventing reading difficulties in young children.* Portsmouth, NH: Heinemann.

Clay, M. M. (2002). *An observation survey of early literacy achievement* (2nd ed.). Portsmouth, NH: Heinemann.

Cohen, J. (1988). *Statistical power analysis for the behavioral sciences* (2nd ed.). Mahwah, NJ: Erlbaum.

Collins, J. (2001). *Good to great: Why some companies make the leap . . . And others don't.* New York, NY: HarperBusiness.

CORE. (1999). *CORE assessing reading: Multiple measures for kindergarten through eighth grade.* Novato, CA: Arena.

Cronbach, L. J. (1942). An analysis of techniques for systematic vocabulary testing. *Journal of Educational Research, 36,* 206–217.

Culham, R. (2010). *Traits of writing: The complete guide for middle school.* New York, NY: Scholastic.

Daywalt, D. (2013). *The day the crayons quit.* New York, NY: Philomel Books.

Dehaene, S. (2009). *Reading in the brain: The science and evolution of a human invention.* New York, NY: Viking.

Deno, S. (1987). Curriculum-based measurement: An introduction. *Teaching Exceptional Children, 20,* 41.

Dolch, E. W. (1948). *Problems in reading.* Champaign, IL: Garrard.

Durkin, D. (1978/1979). What classroom observations reveal about reading comprehension instruction. *Reading Research Quarterly, 15,* 481–533.

Dweck, C. S. (2006). *Mindset: The new psychology of success.* New York, NY: Random House.

Education Trust. (2015). *Checking in: Do classroom assignments reflect today's higher standards? Equity in motion.* Washington, DC: Author.

Fearn, L., & Farnan, N. (2001). *Interactions: Teaching writing and the language arts.* Boston, MA: Houghton Mifflin.

Ferguson, L. E., Bråten, I. I., & Strømsø, H. I. (2012). Epistemic cognition when students read multiple documents containing conflicting scientific evidence: A think-aloud study. *Learning & Instruction, 22*(2), 103–120.

Fisher, D., & Frey, N. (2009). *Background knowledge: The missing piece of the comprehension puzzle.* Portsmouth, NH: Heinemann.

Fisher, D., & Frey, N. (2010). *Enhancing RTI: How to ensure success with effective classroom instruction and intervention.* Alexandria, VA: ASCD.

Fisher, D., & Frey, N. (2012). Close reading in elementary school. *The Reading Teacher, 66*(3), 179–188.

Fisher, D., & Frey, N. (2014). Close reading as an intervention for struggling middle school readers. *Journal of Adolescent and Adult Literacy, 57*(5), 367–376.

Fisher, D., Frey, N., Anderson, H., & Thayre, M. (2015). *Text-dependent questions: Pathways to close and critical reading, grades 6–12.* Thousand Oaks, CA: Corwin.

Fisher, D., Frey, N., & Gonzalez, A. (2010). *Literacy 2.0: Reading and writing in the 21st century.* Bloomington, IN: Solution Tree.

Flanagan, S., & Bouck, E. C. (2015). Mapping out the details: Supporting struggling writers' written expression with concept mapping. *Preventing School Failure, 59*(4), 244–252.

Flavell, J. (1979). Metacognition and cognitive monitoring: A new area of cognitive-developmental inquiry. *American Psychologist, 34,* 906–911.

Flood, J., Lapp, D., & Fisher, D. (2005). Neurological impress method plus. *Reading Psychology, 26,* 147–160.

Frayer, D. A., Frederick, W. C., & Klausmeier, H. J. (1969). *A schema for testing the level of concept mastery (Working paper No. 16).* Madison: Wisconsin Research and Development Center for Cognitive Learning.

Frey, N. (2005). Retention, social promotion, & academic redshirting: What do we know and need to know? *Remedial and Special Education, 26*(6), 332–346.

Frey, N., & Fisher, D. (2009). *Learning words inside and out: Vocabulary instruction that boosts achievement in all subject areas.* Portsmouth, NH: Heinemann.

Frey, N., & Fisher, D. (2013a). A formative assessment system for writing improvement. *English Journal, 103*(1), 66–71.

Frey, N., & Fisher, D. (2013b). *Rigorous reading: Five access points for helping students comprehend complex texts, K–12.* Thousand Oaks, CA: Corwin.

Fuchs, D., Fuchs, L. S., Mathes, P. H., & Simmons, D. C. (1997). Peer-assisted learning strategies: Making classrooms more responsive to diversity. *American Educational Research Journal, 34*(1), 174–206.

Ganske, K. (2000). *Word journeys: Assessment-guided phonics, spelling, and vocabulary instruction.* New York, NY: Guilford.

Ginsburg-Block, M. D., Rohrbeck, C. A., & Fantuzzo, J. W. (2006). A meta-analytic review of social, self-concept, and behavioral outcomes of peer-assisted learning. *Journal of Educational Psychology, 98*(4), 732–749.

Goddard, R. D., Hoy, W. K., & Hoy, A. W. (2000). Collective teacher efficacy: Its meaning, measure, and impact on student achievement. *American Educational Research Journal, 37,* 479–507.

Goodman, Y. M., & Burke, C. L. (1972). *Reading miscue inventory manual: Procedure for diagnosis and evaluation.* New York, NY: Macmillan.

Graham, S., Berninger, V., & Fan, W. (2007). The structural relationship between writing attitude and writing achievement in first and third grade students. *Contemporary Educational Psychology, 32*(3), 516–536.

Graham, S., & Perin, D. (2007). *Writing next: Effective strategies to improve writing of adolescents in middle and high schools.* New York, NY: Carnegie Corporation of New York.

Graves, M. F. (1986). Vocabulary learning and instruction. *Review of Educational Research, 13,* 49–89.

Graves, M. F. (2006). *The vocabulary book: Learning and instruction.* New York, NY: Teachers College.

Guthrie, J., & Klauda, S. (2014). Effects of classroom practices on reading comprehension, engagement, and motivations for adolescents. *Reading Research Quarterly, 49*(4), 387–416.

Guthrie, J. T., & Wigfield, A. (2000). Engagement and motivation in reading. In M. L. Kamil, P. B. Mosenthal, P. D. Pearson, & R. Barr (Eds.), *Handbook of reading research* (Vol. III, pp. 403–424). Mahwah, NJ: Erlbaum.

Hasbrouck, J., & Tindal, G. A. (2006). Oral reading fluency norms: A valuable assessment tool for reading teachers. *Reading Teacher, 59*(7), 636–644.

Hattie, J. (2009). *Visible learning: A synthesis of over 800 meta-analyses relating to achievement.* New York, NY: Routledge.

Hattie, J. (2012). *Visible learning for teachers: Maximizing impact on learning.* New York, NY: Routledge.

Hattie, J. (2014). *The role of learning strategies in today's classrooms.* 34th Vernon Wall Lecture. Retrieved from http://shop.bps.org.uk/publications/publication-by-series/vernon-wall-lecture/34th-vernon-wall-lecture-2014-john-a-c-hattie.html

Hattie, J. (2015). The applicability of visible learning to higher education. *Scholarship of Teaching and Learning in Psychology, 1*(1), 79–91.

Hattie, J. (n.d.). *Visible Learning, that make the difference in education* [PowerPoint presentation]. Visible Learning Laboratories, University of Auckland,

New Zealand. Retrieved from http://docplayer.net/4137828-Visible-learning-that-make-the-difference-in-education-john-hattie-visible-learning-laboratories-university-of-auckland.html

Hattie, J., & Yates, G. (2014). *Visible learning and the science of how we learn.* Oxson, UK: Routledge.

Heckelman, R. G. (1969). A neurological-impress method of remedial-reading instruction. *Academic Therapy, 4,* 277–282.

Henderson, L. L., Weighall, A., & Gaskell, G. (2013). Learning new vocabulary during childhood: Effects of semantic training on lexical consolidation and integration. *Journal of Experimental Child Psychology, 116*(3), 572–592.

Henk, W. A., & Selders, M. L. (1984). Test of synonymic scoring of cloze passages. *The Reading Teacher, 38,* 282–287.

Hoy, W. K., Sweetland, S. R., & Smith, P. A. (2002). Toward an organizational model of achievement in high schools: The significance of collective efficacy. *Educational Administration Quarterly, 38*(1), 77–93.

Hudson, R. F., Lane, H. B., & Pullen, P. C. (2005). Reading fluency assessment and instruction: What, why, and how? *The Reading Teacher, 58,* 702–714.

Hyland, K., & Hyland, F. (Eds.). (2006). *Feedback in second language writing: Contexts and issues.* Cambridge, MA: Cambridge University Press.

Israel, E. (2002). Examining multiple perspectives in literature. In J. Holden & J. S. Schmit (Eds.), *Inquiry and the literary text: Constructing discussions in the English classroom* (pp. 89–103). Urbana, IL: National Council of Teachers of English.

Jacobson, J., Thrope, L., Fisher, D., Lapp. D., Frey, N., & Flood, J. (2001). Cross-age tutoring: A literacy improvement approach for struggling adolescent readers. *Journal of Adolescent & Adult Literacy, 44*(6), 528–536.

Jenkins, S. (2003). *What do you do with a tail like this?* Boston, MA: Houghton Mifflin.

Jerald, C. D. (2007). *Believing and achieving (Issue brief).* Washington, DC: Center for Comprehensive School Reform and Improvement.

Jimerson, S. R. (2001). Meta-analysis of grade retention research: Implications for practice in the 21st century. *School Psychology Review, 30*(3), 420–437.

Johnson, P., & Keier, D. (2011). *Catching readers before they fall.* York, ME: Stenhouse.

Johnson, E., Mellard, D. F., Fuchs, D., & McKnight, M. A. (2006). *Responsiveness to intervention (RTI): How to do it.* Lawrence, KS: National Research Center on Learning Disabilities.

Kahneman, D. (2011). *Thinking fast, thinking slow.* New York, NY: Farrar, Straus and Giroux.

Kear, D. J., Coffman, G. A., McKenna, M. C., & Ambrosio, A. L. (2000). Measuring attitude toward writing: A new tool for teachers. *The Reading Teacher, 54,* 10–23.

Knudson, R. E. (1991). Development and use of a writing attitude survey in grades 4 and 8. *Psychological Reports, 68,* 807–816.

Kuhn, D. (2000). Metacognitive development. *Current Directions in Psychological Science, 9*(5), 178–181.

Kush, J. C., & Watkins, M. W. (1996). Long-term stability of children's attitudes toward reading. *Journal of Educational Research, 89*, 315–319.

LaBerge, D., & Samuels, S. A. (1974). Toward a theory of automatic information processing in reading. *Cognitive Psychology, 6*, 293–323.

Linnenbrink, E. A., & Pintrich, P. R. (2003). The role of self-efficacy beliefs in student engagement and learning in the classroom. *Reading & Writing Quarterly: Overcoming Learning Difficulties, 19*, 119–137.

Lowry, L. (1993). *The giver.* Boston, MA: Houghton Mifflin.

Lublin, J. (2003). *Deep, surface and strategic approaches to learning.* Dublin, Ireland: University College Dublin Centre for Teaching and Learning.

Malloy, J., Marinak, B., Gambrell, L., & Mazzoni, S. (2013). Assessing motivation to read. *Reading Teacher, 67*(4), 273–282.

Marton, F., & Säljö, R. (1976, February). On qualitative differences in learning: 1—Outcome and process. *British Journal of Educational Psychology, 46*(1), pp. 4–11.

Marzano, R. J., & Pickering, D. J. (2005). *Building academic vocabulary: Teacher's manual.* Alexandria, VA: ASCD.

Mathisen, G. E., & Bronnick, K. S. (2009). Creative self-efficacy: An intervention study. *International Journal of Educational Research, 48*, 21–29.

McKenna, M. C., & Kear, D. (1990). Measuring attitude toward reading: A new tool for teachers. *The Reading Teacher, 43*, 626–639.

McNamara, D. S., & Kintsch, W. (1996). Learning from texts: Effects of prior knowledge and text coherence. *Discourse Processes, 22*, 247–282.

Medina, A. L. (2006). Where the beginning ends: Studying leads in literature in order to write attention-getting introductions. *Journal of Adolescent & Adult Literacy, 50*, 190–193.

Michaels, S., O'Connor, M. C., Hall, M. W., & Resnick, L. B. (2010). *Accountable Talk® sourcebook: For classroom conversation that works* (v.3.1). Pittsburgh, PA: University of Pittsburgh Institute for Learning. Retrieved from http://ifl.lrdc.pitt.edu

Mikaelsen, B. (1998). *Petey.* New York, NY: Hyperion Books.

Moore, D. W., & Readence, J. E. (1984). A quantitative and qualitative review of graphic organizer research. *Journal of Educational Research, 71*(1), 11–17.

Murphy, P. K., & Alexander, P. A. (2002). What counts? The predictive powers of subject-matter knowledge, strategic processing, and interest in domain-specific performance. *Journal of Experimental Education, 70*(3), 197–214.

Murphy, P. K., Wilkinson, I. A. G., Soter, A. O., Hennessey, M. N., & Alexander, J. F. (2009). Examining the effects of classroom discussion on students' comprehension of text: A meta-analysis. *Journal of Educational Psychology, 101*(3) 740–764.

Nagy, W. E. (1988). *Teaching vocabulary to improve reading comprehension.* Urbana, IL: National Council of Teachers of English.

Nation, K., & Hulme, C. (1997). Phonemic segmentation, not onset-rime segmentation, predicts early reading and spelling skills. *Reading Research Quarterly, 32,* 154–167.

Nystrand, M. (2006). Research on the role of classroom discourse as it affects reading comprehension. *Research in the Teaching of English, 40,* 392–412.

Palincsar, A. S. (2013). Reciprocal teaching. In J. Hattie & E. Anderman (Eds.), *International guide to student achievement* (pp. 369–371). New York, NY: Routledge.

Palincsar, A. S., & Brown, A. (1984). Reciprocal teaching of comprehension-fostering and comprehension-monitoring activities. *Cognition and Instruction, 1*(2), 117–175.

Paris, S. G. (2005). Reinterpreting the development of reading skills. *Reading Research Quarterly, 40*(2), 184–202.

Paris, S. G., Lipson, M., & Wixson, K. (1983). Becoming a strategic reader. *Contemporary Educational Psychology, 8,* 293–316.

Pauk, W., & Owens, R. J. Q. (2010). *How to study in college* (10th ed.). Boston, MA: Wadworth/Cengage Learning.

Perkins, D. N., & Salomon, G. (1992). Transfer of learning. *International encyclopedia of education* (2nd ed.). Oxford, UK: Pergamon.

Pew Research Center. (2013). E-reading rises as device ownership jumps. Retrieved from http://www.pewinternet.org/files/old-media//Files/Reports/2014/PIP_E-reading_011614.pdf

Poe, E. A. (1843). The tell-tale heart. *The Pioneer.* Philadelphia, PA: James Russell Lowell.

Priebe, S., Keenan, J., & Miller, A. (2012). How prior knowledge affects word identification and comprehension. *Reading & Writing, 25*(1), 131–149.

Protheroe, N. (2008, May). Teacher efficacy: What is it and does it matter? *Principal,* 42–45.

Quindlen, A. (1986, October 21). Love, hate still stew in the new melting pot. *SunSentinel.* Retrieved from http://articles.sun-sentinel.com/1986-10-21/features/8603030958_1_italians-new-jersey-restaurant

Quindlen, A. (2001, September 26). A quilt of a country. *Newsweek.* Retrieved from http://www.newsweek.com/quilt-country-151869

Richards, R. I. (1929). *Practical criticism: A study of literary judgment.* London: Routledge & Kegan Paul.

Rubie-Davies, C. M. (2015). *High and low expectation teachers: The importance of the teacher factor.* New York, NY: Psychology Press.

Ryder, R. J., Burton, J. L., & Silberg, A. (2006). Longitudinal study of direct instruction effects from first through third grade. *Journal of Educational Research, 99*(3), 179–191.

Saki. (n.d.). The interlopers. East of the Web. Retrieved from http://www.eastoftheweb.com/short-stories/UBooks/Inte.shtml

Samuels, S. J. (1979). The method of repeated readings. *The Reading Teacher, 4,* 403–408.

S&S Learning. (2013). A habitat is a home. *Habitats Environment Series*, Grades 4–6. Toronto, ON, Canada: On the Mark Press.

Sapon-Shevin, M. (1994). *Playing favorites: Gifted education and the disruption of community*. Albany: State University of New York Press.

Schmit, J. S. (2002). Different questions, bigger answers: Matching the scope of inquiry to students' needs. In J. Holden & J. S. Schmit (Eds.), *Inquiry and the literary text: Constructing discussion in the English classroom* (pp. 72–78). Urbana, IL: National Council of Teachers of English.

Schmitt, M. B. (1990). A questionnaire to measure children's awareness of strategic reading processes. *The Reading Teacher, 43*, 454–461.

Schwartz, D. L., Chase, C. C., Oppezzo, M. A., & Chin, D. B. (2011). Practicing versus inventing with contrasting cases: The effects of telling first on learning and transfer. *Journal of Educational Psychology, 103*, 759–775.

Shuster, K., & Meany, J. (2005). *Speak out! Debate and public speaking in the middle grades*. New York, NY: International Debate Education Association.

Smith, C. M. (1990). The relationship of adults' reading attitude to actual reading behavior. *Reading Improvement, 27*, 116–121.

Smith, I. (2007). *Sharing learning intentions*. London, UK: Learning Unlimited.

Smith, T. W., Baker, W. K., Hattie, J. A. C., & Bond, L. (2008). A validity study of the certification system of the National Board of Professional Teaching Standards. In L. Ingvarson & J. A. C. Hattie (Eds.), *Assessing teachers for professional certification: The first decade of the National Board of Professional Teaching Standards* (pp. 345–380). Advances in Program Evaluation Series #11. Oxford, UK: Elsevier.

Snell, E. K., Hindman, A. H., & Wasik, B. A. (2015). How can book reading close the word gap? Five key practices from research. *Reading Teacher, 68*(7), 560–571.

Sousa, D. A. (2011). *Educational neuroscience*. Thousand Oaks, CA: Corwin.

Spaulding, C. L. (1992). The motivation to read and write. In J. W. Irwin & M. A. Doyle (Eds.), *Reading/writing connections: Learning from research* (pp. 177–201). Newark, DE: International Reading Association.

Stahl, S. A., & Fairbanks, M. M. (1986). The effects of vocabulary instruction: A model-based meta-analysis. *Review of Educational Research, 56*(1), 72–110.

Stanovich, K. E. (1999). *Who is rational? Studies of individual differences in read*. Mahwah, NJ: Erlbaum.

Stricht, T. G., & James, J. H. (1984). Listening and reading. In P. D. Pearson, R. Barr, M. L. Kamil, & P. Mosenthal (Eds.), *Handbook of reading research* (Vol. 1, pp. 293–317). White Plains, NY: Longman.

Swanson, E., Hairrell, A., Kent, S., Ciullo, S., Wanzek, J. A., & Vaughn, S. (2014). A synthesis and meta-analysis of reading interventions using social studies content for students with learning disabilities. *Journal of Learning Disabilities, 47*(2), 178–195.

Swanson, H. L. (1999a). Reading comprehension and working memory in learning-disabled readers: Is the phonological loop more important than the executive system? *Journal of Experimental Child Psychology, 72*(1), 1–31.

Swanson, H. L. (1999b). Reading research for children with LD: A meta-analysis of intervention outcomes. *Journal of Learning Disabilities, 32*(6), 504–532.

Taylor, W. (1953). Cloze procedure: A new tool for measuring readability. *Journalism Quarterly, 30*, 415–433.

Tierney, R. J., Readance, J., & Dishner, E. (1995). *Reading strategies and practices: A compendium* (4th ed.). Boston, MA: Allyn & Bacon.

Tomlinson, C. A. (2005). *How to differentiate instruction in mixed-ability classrooms.* Alexandria, VA: ASCD.

Topping, K. J. (2006). Building reading fluency: Cognitive, behavioural, and socio-emotional factors and the role of peer-mediated learning (pp. 106–129). In S. J. Samuels & A. E. Farstrup (Eds.), *What research has to say about reading fluency instruction.* Newark, DE: International Reading Association.

Uomini, N. T., & Meyer, G. F. (2013). Shared brain lateralization patterns in language and acheulean stone tool production: A functional transcranial Doppler ultrasound study. *PLoS ONE, 8*(8): e72693. doi:10.1371/journal.pone.0072693.

Van den Broek, P., Tzeng, Y., Risden, K., Trabasso, T., & Basche, P. (2001). Inferential questioning: Effects on comprehension of narrative texts as a function of grade and timing. *Journal of Educational Psychology, 93*(3), 521–529.

Wiggins, G. (1989). The futility of trying to teach everything of importance. *Educational Leadership, 47*(3), 44–59.

Wiggins, G. (1998). *Educative assessment: Designing assessments to inform and improve student performance.* San Francisco, CA: Jossey-Bass.

Wilkinson, I. A. G., & Nelson, K. (2013). Role of discussion in reading comprehension. In J. Hattie & E. Anderman (Eds.), *International guide to student achievement* (pp. 299–302). New York, NY: Routledge.

Wilkinson, P., & Patty, D. (1993). The effects of sentence combining on the reading comprehension of fourth grade students. *Research in the Teaching of English, 27*(1), 104–125.

Winograd, P. N. (1984). Strategic difficulties in summarizing texts. *Reading Research Quarterly, 19*, 404–425.

Wood, T. (1998). Alternative patterns of communication in mathematics classes: funneling or focusing? In H. Steinbring, M. G. Bartolini Bussi, & A. Sierpinska (Eds.), *Language and communication in the mathematics classroom* (pp. 167–78). Reston, VA: National Council of Teachers of Mathematics.

Wylie, R. E., & Durrell, D. D. (1970). Teaching vowels through phonograms. *Elementary English, 47*, 787–791.

Yamada, K. (2013). *What do you do with an idea?* Seattle, WA: Compendium.

Yopp, H. K. (1995). A test for assessing phonemic awareness in young children. *The Reading Teacher, 49*, 20–29.

Index

Notes

Notes

Notes

A SAGE Publishing Company

Helping educators make the greatest impact

CORWIN HAS ONE MISSION: to enhance education through intentional professional learning.

We build long-term relationships with our authors, educators, clients, and associations who partner with us to develop and continuously improve the best evidence-based practices that establish and support lifelong learning.

visible learning^{plus}

3 Ways to Get Started

1. Understand Your Baseline

School Capability Analysis

How does your school measure against the five strands of Visible Learning? Certified consultants will conduct a half-day site visit to collect and analyze baseline capability data to determine your school's readiness for Visible Learning^{plus}. A full written report is provided.

The Foundation Series

Begin your Visible Learning^{plus} journey by building your team's foundational knowledge of the Visible Learning research. Teachers and school leaders will receive tools for gathering evidence of effective practice and create a plan for making learning visible for all students.

2. Build Foundational Knowledge

3. Drive Whole-System Reform

Seminars
Training
Consulting

Collaborative Impact Program

The Collaborative Impact program is our gold standard for sustainable reform, as it aligns system leaders, school leaders, and teachers with a proven process to build capacity for change over 3-5 years, with measurable results.

Contact your account manager at (800) 831-6640 or visit www.corwin.com/visiblelearning

CORWIN
A SAGE Publishing Company

CORWIN LITERACY

Gretchen Bernabei & Judi Reimer

On 101 lessons and mentor texts for tackling the most persistent issues in academic writing

Gretchen Bernabei

On 101 lessons to help students master the conventions of grammar and usage once and for all

Douglas Fisher, Nancy Frey & Diane Lapp

On how to use complexity as a dynamic, powerful tool for using right text at just the right time

Douglas Fisher, Nancy Frey, & John Hattie

On identifying the instructional routines that have the biggest impact on student learning

Douglas Fisher & Nancy Frey

On five access points for seriously stretching students' capacity to comprehend complex text

Douglas Fisher & Nancy Frey

On how text-dependent questions can inspire close and critical reading, grades K–5 & 6–12

To order your copies, visit **www.corwin.com/literacy**